ONE MINUTE
OF PRAISE

The Most Powerful Minute of Your Day

Pastor Darlene McCarty

Legacy Publishers International
Denver, Colorado

ISBN: 1-880809-64-8

Published in Denver, Colorado, by Legacy Publishers International

Manuscript prepared by Melissa Killian, Killian Creative, Boulder, Colorado. www.killiancreative.com

Library of Congress Cataloging-in-Publication Data

13 12 11 10 09 08 07   3 4 5 6 7 8 9 10 11 12

Dedication

Chase Walker Whitehurst

12/22/02 - 4/24/06

To a precious angel sent to visit with us for three beautiful years. Chase may have carried a burden with his special needs, but he was never a burden to carry. You will always have a special place in Nana and Papa's heart and you will be greatly missed. We called you Chase because we prayed as you grew, you would always be a God chaser. It never entered our minds that you would chase God so passionately, that you would catch Him at such an early age. I love you!

One Minute of Praise

Acknowledgments

First and foremost I dedicate the words pinned to the pages in this book to my Lord and Savior. Father: where would I be without Him? Let me take this opportunity to say, "Thank you Lord for choosing this vessel to house your precious anointing."

To my faithful, loving, and precious husband Randel, who for the past thirty-six years has encouraged me to launch into the destiny that God has created for me. Sweetheart, your unquestionable love to the Lord and me as your wife has set a high standard that both of our daughters, Tyra and Tiffany choose to follow in their ministry and their companions, Jason and Paul. Thank you for not just preaching the Word from the pulpit, but for living it at home as well.

 Acknowledgements

To my daughter Tyra and her husband Jason Whitehurst to whom God has placed a call of the ministry upon their life. Thank you for answering that call with a willing heart. I have seen in your life, no matter if your day begins with sunshine or a storm, that your dedication to His calling does not waver.

To my second daughter Tiffany and her husband Paul Strong. What an honor to have two daughters in full-time ministry. Your example as a passionate and anointed leader rises above the heads of others. The call of God burns like a torch in your soul. Man did not place it there, so therefore do not let man extinguish that flame from your spirit.

To three woman that have had a big impact on my life. Thank you Pastor Paula White, Pastor Darlene Bishop, and Prophetess Juanita Bynum first of all for pouring the passion of the Lord and the wisdom of the Word into me through your ministry. Secondly, for acknowledging the call of God upon my life and opening new doors for me to pass through.

To my friend Mike Rogers with Supernatural Finances Ministries who taught me the 7 steps to living a blessed life. Step #1: Loving God for 1 minute each day. My loving God turned into praise and my 1 minute turned into multiple minutes per day.

To the staff of Legacy Publishers International, for believing in a message that was in my heart and putting it on paper for the world to read. Thank you Bishop Dennis and Michelle Leonard, Dawn Miller, and Melissa Killian for taking a dream and bringing it to life.

Endorsements

"As a writer, Darlene McCarty is not just on the cutting edge, but more accurately – she *is* the cutting edge. Her writing is timely and expedient, written for the willing hearted, those who are not afraid to be confronted with life-changing truth. Darlene continues to produce pertinent material for a pertinent generation."

Evangelist Dave Roever, D.D.
President of Roever and Associates, Fort Worth, Texas
www.daveroever.org

"You cannot read this book without being changed. Praise will change you and your circumstances. In Darlene's wonderful and unique style, she will stir again the passion for praise in your life and bring great charity to its priority and value."

Karen Wheaton
Karen Wheaton Ministries, Minister / Recording Artist

"It is refreshing to watch how God has transformed Darlene McCarty. She has always been a faithful Pastor's wife, an excellent musician, a nurturing mother and a role model for ladies in the parsonage. But over the last 5 years the Lord has energized her life with a fresh anointing and a new ministry assignment. I have always known Darlene as a loyal helpmate of her husband's ministry and the faithful prayer warrior behind the scenes, yet today the Lord of the harvest is moving her from the parsonage to the platform with a dynamic word for the church.

The Lord has revealed to Darlene key secrets concerning praise. Those secrets she has walked out in life and ministry and the results are evident in her home, marriage, family and personal life.

Though the book is entitled *One Minute of Praise*, these truths will fill your life with hours of intimacy with the Lord."

I thank the Lord for Darlene and Randel daily."

Edward Turner
Superintendent for the Tennessee
District Council of the Assemblies of God
Nashville, Tennessee

"This is a must read! Darlene McCarty has put together powerful insights that will have you laughing, crying, and most importantly—growing. Darlene knows the power of praise! This book will open your eyes, unlock your heart and fill your spirit. Don't wait another minute—dig in today! It will change your life!"

Martha Munizzi
Martha Munizzi Ministries / Recording Artist
Orlando, Florida

One Minute of Praise

"I have known Pastor Darlene McCarthy for about 3 years. She is a woman of prayer and consecration. This coupled with her love for giving praise to God has given her the divine power to write *One Minute of Praise* with passion. *One Minute of Praise* will encourage you, inspire you and give you a joy that surpasses all understanding. Once you have begun your One Minute of Praise you will be sparked to lead a life time of exalting the almighty. *One Minute of Praise* is an awesome source of inspiration."

Dr. Yvonne Capehart
Sister Keeper Ministries, Pensacola, Florida

"This book practically and effectively speaks to the power of praise in the life of a Christian. The author possesses a thorough knowledge and grasp of Scripture along with a life-time of personal experience in living out these biblical truths."

Kermit S. Bridges, D. Min., President
Southwestern Assemblies of God University
Waxahachie, Texas

"Darlene McCarty in her book, *One Minute of Praise*, created something in the spirit through revelation knowledge that every believer can do. Praise is comely (natural) the Psalmist David said in Psalms 33:1 (KJV). So when we open our mouth and begin to shout out praise to God, even for one minute-the enemy is destroyed and all of Hell is paralyzed when we make a choice to praise Him regardless. A quick read, very handy and practical."

Judy Jacobs
Minister / Recording Artist, His Song Ministries
Cleveland, Tennessee

"As I read this book I felt an extreme desire to weep in the presence of Jesus. Darlene has captured the heart of the Father for the turning of the church from religion to intimacy. She has with her words shouldered a burden of relentless pursuit of the true heart of a worshiper. I laughed as I read this book, because I could see Darlene preaching with intensity and power as only she can this life changing message. This book will revolutionize lives to go to a higher level if freedom in Christ! She has so many times changed our student's lives, our staff's lives, and Karen's and my life! You did it again Darlene! Thank you Darlene for realness which always births reverence for more of our Savior!"

Patrick H. Schatzline
President of Mercy Seat Ministries, and
The Forerunner School of Ministry
Birmingham, Alabama

"Darlene McCarty has written a book so simple, yet so life changing. If we could all take just one minute and focus strictly on God and give him the praise he deserves, we would all be closer to God. Can it really be this simple? Darlene reveals in her book how this easy task could change your life forever! I encourage you to take time to read this inspirational book and see how it changes your life."

Mike Rogers
President, Rogers Consulting Ltd. Co.
Founder of Supernatural Finances
Lubbock, Texas

"Prayer is my life, and in Darlene McCarty's book, *One Minute of Praise*, she so accurately states that your praise is your password into the Throne Room. You can't enter into prayer except you come with a praise in your mouth! The words of your mouth will either announce your next victory or pronounce your next defeat. Your victory is on the other side of your praise and this book will drive you so that your *One Minute of Praise* turns into hours spent in His presence."

Pastor Darlene Bishop
Solid Rock Church, Monroe, Ohio

"A charming book on the power of praise has over Satan's attempt to discourage and defeat. Bible-based and Heaven-sent, this book is a must-read for anyone seeking closer fellowship with Christ. The chapter on extreme praise gives the believer insight regarding coming into the presence of the Lord with sincerity and enthusiasm."

Dr. James L. Davis
Vice President for Development
Southeastern University, Lakeland, Florida

"Life without 'PRAISE' is a life that is Empty. Thank God for Darlene's book that emphasizes the power and dynamics of Praise."

Dr. Steve L. Brock
Steve Brock Ministries/Benny Hinn Ministries
Dacula, Georgia

One Minute of Praise

Table of Contents

Foreword

*O*ne of the most powerful points of access we have into the very presence of God is praise. Every single time we lift our voices and hearts in praise, we get God's attention; His focus becomes directed towards us and our hearts' desires. In that moment, He opens up the Heavens and pours His spirit upon us, granting peace and comfort and strength when we need it most.

The Word of God says that our praise is as *"a sweet smell, a sacrifice acceptable, well pleasing to God"*. The simple act of praise is one of the most valuable sacrifices that God recognizes. He rewards that sacrifice by pouring more of Himself into our lives.

How often do you use this supernatural key to gain access to His presence? How much time do you invest in getting closer to God, and drawing Him closer to you? Sure, we all call upon Him in times of despair - when our needs are greater than our resources. But what about just loving on God with holy abandon? What about dedicating time - even if only a minute - to expressions of love and admiration and exaltation to the God of Heaven and Earth? What about setting aside our own selfish desires to spend time exclaiming His worth and deity and goodness?

Can *One Minute of Praise* change your life? You bet it can! Sixty seconds of focused energy spent thanking, honoring, pleasing God – not asking, not questioning, not complaining – can change your situation. Pastor Darlene McCarty has captured the value of simple, pure praise in this gem of a book. She has taken the sometimes larger than life concept of praise and worship to a level of tangibility that anyone can receive and begin to act upon today.

Can you spare *One Minute of Praise* to change your life? You can't afford not to!

~Pastor Paula White

One Minute of Praise

Introduction

*T*oday, you have a choice that will alter the course of your life. You can either choose—as most do—to move from one level to the next, or you can choose to move from where you are now to another dimension. Stair stepping from level to level is going from one to two, or two to three. It is a life of incremental improvement—it is often safe, comfortable, and controllable. But moving to another dimension is transferring beyond the realm of levels—and doing that which will require you to do something that you have never done before. It is to place yourself fully in the hands of God—and when you do that, only God knows the miracles that might take place.

Choosing to start your day with **"One Minute of Praise"** is to choose this second path. Living by praise is not a feeling that is going to fall on you or something that will hit you up beside the head. Praising is something you must do on purpose. No matter your circumstances, you have the choice to tap into the conduit that connects you to the Throne Room or stay right where you are defeated, beaten up, and bogged down with the burdens in your world. Praise is that conduit.

Psalms 118:24 KJV says, *"This is the day which the Lord has made; we will rejoice and be glad in it."* When David spoke this, it wasn't because he woke up to an overwhelmingly beautiful day. I believe this is a declaration of King David's faith. I'm sure he did not feel like praising that day, but he knew he had a choice to either praise his Lord or be overcome by his circumstances, and he decided to choose praise. We have the same choice to make every morning.

If you want to be a full-time overcomer, however, you have to decide to praise God whether you feel like it or not—you cannot rely on feelings to determine when and where you give God praise. Ultimately, there are only two opportunities to let praise fill your mouth. When you feel like it and when you don't. If you let your feelings make this choice, you will be subject to whatever happens around you.

When life's circumstances start to discourage you, choose like David,

I will praise the LORD at all times. I will constantly speak his praises. I will boast only in the LORD; let all who are discouraged take heart. Come, let us tell of the LORD's greatness; let us exalt his name together.

Psalms 34:1-3

One Minute of Praise

God promises great blessings to His people, but blessings require active participation. He will set you free from your fears, protect your household, rescue you from your enemies, show you goodness, supply your needs, and redeem you from the sins of this world—when you keep heaven open over you and your home.

If you're asking, "How do I access this life-giving power?" then you've made the right choice by opening this book. I will take you into a deeper understanding from God's Word concerning the power that is already within you. The most precious gift that you possess can invade hell and excite heaven, but you have to release it. It takes intentional participation for God to invade your territory. He needs you to open the door: Your circumstances need not determine your destiny, but your praise can. On the good days and on the days when all hell breaks loose, your password into His presence is Praise. Praise covers you with a fragrance that is pleasing to the King. Your praise brings you favor and immediate access into His Throne Room.

I pray this book opens new dimensions of God's grace to you as you begin to enter and live everyday in new realms of praise—one minute at a time.

Let the journey begin!

Darlene McCarty
Memphis, Tennessee

 Introduction

One Minute of Praise

I.

Praise Lifts You Out of Your Valley

ONE

Praise and Faith

And the Holy Spirit helps us in our distress. For we don't even know what we should pray for, nor how we should pray. But the Holy Spirit prays for us with groanings that cannot be expressed in words.

Romans 8:26

It's Monday morning at 5:45 a.m. on April 24, 2006. Suddenly, I'm awakened by the sound of my telephone ringing. I look at the caller ID—it is my daughter Tyra calling from her home in Nashville. What I heard as I answered the phone sent my world into a tailspin. My mind reeled as the blood rushed to my head. I felt sick to my stomach and hoped desperately that I was only dreaming and would soon wake up.

But it was not a dream. I heard the sound of my daughter in panic. It's a sound that I go to bed with every night, playing over and over in my ears. I hear, "Mama, Mama, Chase is dead!" I said, "Who, what?" She screams franticly, "Jason went upstairs to Chase's bedroom and he is dead."

I put the phone on speakerphone and handed it to my husband and began to sob and pray in the Spirit. I was three and a half hours away and my daughter needed me—and I could not be there soon enough to hold and comfort her.

What do you do when your back is against the wall, you don't know what to pray, and there is nowhere to turn?

All that I could do was moan and groan in the Spirit.

Chase, our grandson, was born three and a half years ago on December 22, 2002 at twenty-nine weeks weighing only two pounds, ten ounces. The doctors told us his lungs were extremely underdeveloped and did not give us much hope for his survival. Along with many area churches, our family began to pray for him. His breathing began to improve hour by hour. The doctors were quite surprised when a lung x-ray showed his lungs fully developed compared to the first x-ray where his lungs only went down to his 4th rib. God had performed a miracle in Chase. But at three-days-old, we were told that Chase had a rare heart defect, an Arota-pulmonary window. The cardiologist did not believe he would survive until the surgery.

Through many ups and downs, Chase made it to the five-pound mark required for open-heart surgery. The surgery was a success and Chase's heart did not suffer any complications from the wait. God had completed another miracle in Chase. What the cardiologists didn't know was that the entire time that Chase was in the hospital, Jason and Tyra were reading healing scriptures to him and singing praises over him. We understood the power in God's Word and praise. Chase was sent home from the hospital with a clean bill of health—there was not any need for either a breathing or heart machine.

At ten-months-old, Chase developed seizures. When the seizures started, his slow physical development slowed even more. We praised God everyday for Chase being healed of his seizures. Every night as Jason and Tyra would lay him in his bed, they would thank God that one day Chase would walk, talk, and be a mighty man of God. They continually let praise come from their lips for Chase's healing, growth, and development. Circumstance did not steal their faith in God. They knew what God was capable of doing and the enemy was not going to deceive them into believing otherwise.

Soon after, a doctor in St. Louis introduced Jason and Tyra to a special diet that helped them control Chase's seizures. He was doing so well. As the seizures began decreasing his growth and development began increasing. Chase would go days without a seizure. As of April 24, 2006,

Chase had gone three weeks without any seizures. God's faithfulness seemed overwhelming at that point.

I pray that you never lose sight of the goodness and faithfulness of God.

Holy Spirit, remind us daily of Your mercy and love. Help us to rest in Your grace and allow Your peace to ever guard our hearts and minds. Spirit of Truth, make us mindful of Your Presence and help us in every situation to be still and know that You alone are God.

One Minute of Praise:

No matter the circumstances, never lose sight of the victories. Remind yourself of the many times that God has proven Himself faithful and praise Him that His mercies are new every morning—stir up a grateful heart as you enter into His gates for one minute of praise.

_____

_____

_____

_____

_____

TWO

Out of the Mouth of Babes

*O Lord, our Lord, how majestic is your name in all
the earth! You have set your glory above heavens.
Out of the mouth of babes and infants, you have
established strength because of your foes, to still the
enemy and the avenger.*

Psalm 8:1,2 ESV

*I*f you have ever been through the death of a loved one,
you understand the places you have to go and the
decisions you have to make. In the days following, you will

go to the hardest places emotionally you have ever been, and make the most difficult decisions of your life. Your emotions are on a roller coaster ride. You can be laughing one moment and losing it the next. The reality of what has just happened hits you, the blood rushes to your head, you feel sick to your stomach, and you think, "If I could only turn the clock back maybe I could undo what has happened." Your mind begins to think, "Maybe I'm just asleep. I'm having a bad dream and when I wake up everything will be okay." Then you realize you are not asleep and the roller coaster ride of the mind starts all over again.

When we arrived at our daughter's and son-in-law's house in Nashville, I ran to Tyra standing in the kitchen. She fell to the floor and when I reached over to pick her up it was as if I was picking up my little girl who had fallen down so many times when she was younger. I remembered how I would kiss her hurt, put a band-aid on it, and everything would be okay. But this time was different.

All I could do was hold her, cry with her, and say, "Baby, I know it hurts so badly. It's okay to cry. I'm here and I love you." All I could do was say these same words over and over and over. Ever been some place where there are no words to express what is going on inside of you? That is where I was. What do you say to your thirty-two-year-old daughter who had an unexpected visit from the angel of death? At such a point, only God can reach down and kiss the heart of a broken mother and father and bring healing to their emotions. One thing I know about my Heavenly Father, He never leaves us or forsakes us.

The time from when Chase was taken from Jason's and Tyra's arms until we said good-bye to him at the cemetery seemed like one long nightmare. The question "Why?" keeps popping into your head. You begin to tell God all the reasons this should not have happened. You quote every scripture you know trying to find comfort. You say every prayer you know trying to find answers.

You know that God is Who He says He is—and He is there with you—but at that moment you feel it just isn't fair. You had faith in your heart that God would heal. You thanked God every day for healing and complete restoration. Perhaps you have been a Christian your entire life, or like me, it might be that everyone in your family is a minister or married to a preacher. You yourself may have preached healing and witnessed miracles, but now all you know is the tragedy before you. You ask, "What have we done to deserve this? Why God, why?"

Chase's six-year-old sister Mackenzie described it best. She asked Jason, "Can God bring Chase back to life like He did when he was born?" Jason replied, "Chase has gone to live with Jesus. When Chase was born he never did die. He was just very sick." She thought for a few minutes and in her sweet, tender voice said, "Oh, I get it. When Chase was born he had a race to run and yesterday God said to Chase,

'Chase you have finished your race. It's time for you to come and live with me.'"

No wonder Jesus loved hanging around children. Children see things sometimes we adults don't have the simple understanding to see.

Within a few hours of Chase's death, people from all around the world began to call the house or our cell phones. Youth Evangelist Reggie Dabbs called while doing a youth conference in Australia. Missionaries Keith and Christy Jones called from Jordan. Pastor Paula White called from a conference in Los Angeles. Pastor Darlene Bishop and Singer/Preacher Judy Jacobs called and prayed for us over the phone. I am so thankful to God for placing people in our lives that brought strength from around the world. God had people in place to hold our arms up when we were too weak to stand.

Lord, help me to be more "simpleminded" to see Your beauty in the difficult times, to experience Your grace during life's most challenging moments, and especially to daily find joy in the simplest of pleasures.

One Minute of Praise:

Focus on the little things, the small delights, and that for which you can be grateful even in the rough places.

_____

_____

_____

_____

_____

_____

_____

THREE

Strengthened by Praise

Be still, and know that I am God. I will be exalted among the nations, I will be exalted in the earth!

Psalm 46:10 ESV

The days following our grandson's death, we knew what we had to do to survive. It would come through prayer, the Word, and our praise. When we couldn't sleep we would either pray, read the Word, or speak forth praise. Every night when we went to bed, I praised myself to sleep. When I was awakened during the night, it's praise that put me back to sleep. Even though it has not been an easy road, God's grace never left us. Each day grew slowly better.

The Lord graciously gave us comfort through words from friends, dreams, and visions. Two and a half weeks after

Chase's death, Jason, Tyra, and Mackenzie picked up one of Mackenzie's friends on Wednesday night and took her to church with them. After church they drove into the apartment complex where her little friend lived. Jason parked and walked the two girls up to the apartment. The mother came outside and talked with Jason while the two girls played. As Tyra was sitting in the car waiting on Jason and Mackenzie to return, suddenly a vision appeared to her. She saw a car hit Mackenzie. It frightened her so badly, she immediately began to look around the parking lot for Mackenzie. As she looked in front of her, she saw an SUV approaching, while at the same time she saw Mackenzie running toward her. She was about to run in-between the parked cars which meant the SUV would not see her until she ran out in front of it. The thought rushed through her mind, "Would God take both of my children within two weeks?"

The back passenger side of their car was opened and as loud as Tyra could scream, she yelled, "Stop Mackenzie." When Mackenzie and the SUV stopped, they were within a foot from each other.

At that moment, Tyra said she heard a soft voice say to her, "You see, I have the power of life and death in my hand." She knew to whom that voice belonged because she had heard it before. She knew the Lord loved her enough to give her confirmation that it was no accident that Chase had died and she was not to blame herself or feel guilty for not being with him. She knew God had it all under control.

God had given her a peace that started a healing in her that can only come from Him. The "why" and the "what for" were no longer important.

Even though we still miss Chase and always will, there is no anger or disappointment towards God. He knows exactly where we are and how much we can bear. God knows what is inside each one of us, and what needs to be developed and cultivated in our lives. It's through the tough times that God develops our character and who we are in Him.

Thank You, Father God, for being mindful of the needs and abilities of each one of us. Thank You for Your watchfulness and affection toward us. We know that there is nothing that happens without Your foreknowledge nor outside Your divine wisdom. Thank You for Your comfort and peace that transcends our limited understanding of Your amazing grace.

One Minute of Praise:

Take a moment to rest in the knowledge of God. Quiet your mind and be still. As you wait contentedly on the peace of God to surround you, remember His goodness, meditate on His trustworthiness, and write what comes to mind.

FOUR

Surprised by Praise

I will bless the Lord at all times; his praise shall continually be in my mouth. My soul makes its boast in the Lord; let the humble hear and be glad. Oh, magnify the Lord with me, and let us exalt his name together!

Psalm 34:1-3 NEV

Growing up Tyra wrestled with the insecurity of what others thought of her. The sun rose and set on people's opinions of her. This obstacle in her life was a hindrance to fulfilling her Godly potential, but when Chase was born, because of his special needs such as eyeglasses and a special stroller, people would look and stare. I know they didn't mean any harm, but their attention was very uncomfortable for Tyra. The looks that she had to deal with began a healing process. Soon, people's opinions were no longer important to her. All that mattered was what God thought.

In her devotional time, she began to seek a deeper understanding of God's Word. Her prayer life increased in its fervency. She developed insight into God's grace, and more often than not, words of praise were coming out of her mouth. She is not the same woman she had been three and a half years earlier when Chase was born. She loved and served God before, but now there was a deeper conse-cration in her daily relationship with her Heavenly Father.

When Tyra was pregnant with Chase, she had a dream about Chase and Mackenzie. She saw Chase running to her with Mackenzie running close behind him. He jumped up into her arms and said, "Mommy, I love you so much." In her dream, Mackenzie was six and Chase was three. We had always confidently believed for Chase's healing because Tyra saw him perfect and whole. Mackenzie is now six, and Chase had turned three in December of 2005. Little did we realize that only a few months into 2006, his perfection would ultimately be realized in heaven. We praise God for caring enough that he sent this little angel to teach us what no other person could.

As a result, we have learned to give God praise for the little things in life. We remember applauding Chase when he pushed and pushed and forced his head up and looked around knowing this was a victory for him. We constantly told him he was a mighty man of God and he was going to be a preacher someday. Even though preparing took a long time because of his special diet and he had to be taken to therapy four times a week, Chase was never a burden. He was a blessing! Little Chase may have carried a burden, but he was never a burden to carry.

Isn't that just like our Heavenly Father? His Son, Jesus Christ carried our burdens to the cross so that we would not have a burden to carry ourselves.

I have learned to praise Him in the wonderful times and through the tough times. As I wrote this book, I did not just write what I had read in other books—even though good Christian books are needed for encouragement; but I wrote what I have lived through, survived, and can shout about. Yes, praise be to God, we're still standing and giving Him glory!

Our grandson was named Chase because we knew he was called to be a God Chaser. Little did we know while listening to his Benny Hinn Healing CDs in the hospital or at home, that the Lord would actually catch Him up at such an early age to receive his perfected body in heaven.

Isaiah 61:3 KJV comforts us with these words, "to give unto them beauty for ashes, the oil of joy for mourning, the garment of praise for the spirit of heaviness; that they might be called trees of righteousness, the planting of the Lord, that he might be glorified."

I have learned that when trouble comes, sometimes God carries us through it, sometimes He helps us in it, sometimes He keeps us from it; but even though He may allow us to experience pain, one thing is for sure, He will never allow us to be defeated.

Praise you Lord for Your steadfast love—for Your infinite goodness and boundless mercy. There is no pain too great, or sorrow so deep, that You cannot reach it with your comfort and healing. You are a God of restoration, redemption, and resurrection life. Thank You, Lord, for Your new mercies every morning, for restoring broken hearts, relieving troubled minds, and renewing our hope in You.

One Minute of Praise:

What are your deepest hurts? What is your greatest hope? Stir up your faith by declaring the hope you have in Him to meet every need, heal every hurt, and fulfill every dream.

_____

_____

_____

_____

_____

II.

Praise Brings Victory

FIVE

The Power to Change

Jesus looked at them and said, With man this is impossible, but with God all things are possible.

Matthew 19:26 ESV

*S*itting in front of my TV in my family room, little did I know that the Lord was about to work me over! I had just returned from doing a taping with the esteemed Juanita Bynum at Trinity Broadcasting Network in Atlanta. I was going to critique myself, completely unaware that this wasn't going to be about what I thought—but God was going to tell me what *He* thought.

As I watched the program and listened to myself minister, the Lord spoke softly, but bluntly to me. He said, "Do you see the anointing that I have placed upon you?" I agreed with Him on that part. But the next statement blew me away. It would change my life forever. He said, "You have prepared yourself spiritually to carry my anointing, but you have not prepared yourself physically to carry my anointing. The places I want to take you, you cannot go because you are too overweight to get there. You cannot keep up with the schedule that I have designed for you. You choose today which road you will take. Your choice will determine your destiny."

Talk about taking your breath away, knocking the props out from underneath you, slapping you in the face, and hurling you into reality—that did it! God was right. For the past nine years I had become so passionate for God and His Word—I was growing by leaps and bounds in Him—I was going places I had never been and meeting Godly people that I had never met before. I knew it was God and He was right. I huffed and puffed walking down the corridor at the airport and would have to sit down to catch my breath. I couldn't eat before I spoke because I wouldn't be able to breathe. I couldn't sleep on my back because I would wake up gasping for air.

You might ask the question, "Why did you continue to live this way?" It's simple. I hated the way I looked. I disliked how I felt. I dreaded going on long trips because my feet would hurt. But I learned to tolerate this lifestyle. What you can tolerate you will never change. It makes no difference how much you hate something—it might be a relationship, a marriage, a job, or your attitude—but as long as you tolerate it, you will not change.

After having the Holy Spirit speak to me the way He did, I knew God's will for the rest of my life would be determined by the decision I made that evening. I told the Lord if He would help me, I would help myself and I would develop my body into a vessel of honor that would bring glory to Him. I had reached a point in my life that I no longer could tolerate what I was and I chose to change.

I was, fifty-five-years-old, and I had battled a weight problem my entire life. Now I was determined to conquer something that I had never been able to conquer before, and suddenly I realized I had a new advantage—GOD!

Praise had become such a big part of my life. I had learned to never underestimate the importance of praise. I knew it was one of the most powerful spiritual weapons I had at my disposal. Praise had become more than a song with a few uplifting words about the Lord. I had learned my praise releases the very presence of God Himself. I also knew that when the presence of God comes to dwell with me, my enemies have to retreat. I knew that every weak area in my life had to flee when it was faced with my joy-filled praise. I knew praise held the key to my victory.

Thank You, Lord God, that you found it fitting to inhabit the praises of your people. When You are inhabiting our very words, certainly no temptation, challenge, or problem is so great that Your Presence can't bring change and success. May all we speak bring You praise and glory—and bring us victory!

One Minute of Praise:

Hallelujah! What a hope we have in Him! What powerful weapons of warfare we have at our disposal to send our enemies fleeing! No temptation, no challenge, no issue is immune to the life-giving presence of God that fills our praises. Meditate on that, and write down what comes to mind.

_____

_____

_____

_____

_____

_____

_____

_____

_____

_____

SIX

The Praise Diet

Then Jonah prayed to the Lord his God from inside the fish. He said, "I cried out to the Lord in my great trouble, and he answered me. I called to you from the world of the dead, and Lord, you heard me! You threw me into the ocean depths, and I sank down to the heart of the sea. I was buried beneath your wild and stormy waves. Then I said, `O Lord, you have driven me from your presence. How will I ever again see your holy Temple?'

"I sank beneath the waves, and death was very near. The waters closed in around me, and seaweed wrapped itself around my head. I sank down to the very roots of the mountains. I was locked out of life

and imprisoned in the land of the dead. But you, O Lord my God, have snatched me from the yawning jaws of death!

When I had lost all hope, I turned my thoughts once more to the Lord. And my earnest prayer went out to you in your holy Temple. Those who worship false gods turn their backs on all God's mercies. But I will offer sacrifices to you with songs of praise, and I will fulfill all my vows. For my salvation comes from the Lord alone.

Then the Lord ordered the fish to spit up Jonah on the beach, and it did.

Jonah 2:1-20

*A*s I read the story of Jonah in the belly of the whale, I noticed something interesting. In verses two through eight he is praying to God, but in verse nine his prayer changes. It says he sang praise. Out of his mouth came praise. One song of praise did more than three days of whining and complaining about his circumstances.

If praise can propel a fish to dry land and cause it to spit out a man so he could do the will of his God Jehovah, then I knew my praise could spit me out of a whale called fat and start me on my journey to do the will of the same God.

I knew God had not changed his mind or backed-out on the destiny that He had called me to fulfill. He was just waiting on me. I knew my calling was irrevocable and irreversible and if I did not heed His call I would be out of the will of God. Although I might use all the excuses in the book about why I could not do what God wanted me to do—being overweight was not an excuse in God's book. He was just waiting on me to catch up with Him.

Through His Word I knew that God had equipped me to handle all the challenges that were before me. He told me in First Corinthians 10:13 that He would not allow anything to come upon me that would be more than I could handle. So if I can handle it, then I know He has equipped me with what I need to be an overcomer.

I determined within myself that God had a purpose for my life and through my prayer and praise I was going to get there. I told God if He would do His part in helping me get my weight off, I could do my part. So I got up every morning praising God that I was going to make it through breakfast. When I wanted a snack, I praised the Lord for helping me choose a healthy snack. I praised Him through my lunchtime and my praise continued through the afternoon until supper. Through my praise, God gave me the strength to make the right choices. If I messed up and fell, I got back up and started from where I left off, praising Him the whole way through.

As a result, eating healthy has become a lifestyle not a diet. On a diet you lose the pounds just to put them back on—plus more—when you are off it again. Believe me, I've been there and done that! Now I'm an avid label reader on all the food I buy at the grocery store. I have discovered what works best for me is to watch my fat grams. I also set up an accountability relationship with a friend. I weigh in with her every month. When I am having a rough day, she encourages me. As I lose weight she congratulates me for my success.

Accountability is so important. You think twice about cheating. Whatever God can use as a tool outside of praise to help you get control of your eating habits, use it. Whether you learn from a person, a weight program, a book, or teaching series on weight control, educate yourself. Pray and ask the Lord for guidance and wisdom.

The most powerful tool that I have, though, is praise. My Heavenly Father walks with me, talks to me, encourages me, tells me I can make it, and promises me He will never leave me—and He has kept His word.

I lost seventy pounds in less than a year. Though I have twenty-five more to go, I know I can make it because I am not walking this road alone. God wants me at my best.

The next time the devil tries to brainwash you with failure, turn him back with your powerful weapon of praise. Lift your voice, your hands, and your heart to God and shout your praise until it lifts the roof. Your willpower will strengthen, and your decision-making will improve, and your self-worth will return. You will be so proud of yourself because you have become an overcomer.

Lord, I pray that those who have allowed their weight to hinder them from doing Your will would be pushed into a no tolerance zone. Don't let them continue to live where they are. Allow them to be miserable for compromising. I speak health into their body and mind. Jesus, Your body upon the cross bore every temptation. Heavenly Father, encourage them right now that they can make a change and a difference no matter how overweight they are or how old or young they might be. I speak forth life and vitality in Jesus name. Amen!

One Minute of Praise:

What is keeping you from being all you can be in Christ—and for Christ? Whatever your obstacles, praise Him now for helping you to overcome them. With God's help, you *will* succeed! Praise Him for His help and for your eminent success!

SEVEN

The Key to Victory

*Now thanks be to God who always leads us in tri-
umph in Christ, and through us diffuses the fragrance of His knowledge in every place.*

2 Corinthians 2:14 NKJV

W hy should I expect victory every time? Just because I
speak it doesn't mean I believe it—that I really, really
believe it. It might be easier for me to believe for you because
it's your problem and not my problem. But when they've
diagnosed me with cancer and I have tumors all over my
body, then can I sincerely say, I must choose to B-E-L-I-E-V-E.
Bishop Darlene Bishop says it like this, "**B**ecause **E**mmanuel
Lives **I** **E**xpect **V**ictory **E**verytime." We find out what we're
really made out of during those times when we've had our

back against the wall—when our pain is personal or life threatening—then God sees what our praise is made of.

As I began to study this, I asked the Lord, "What is my key to victory? Lord, what can I give as the key element— what can I tell them is the key to victory every time? What is the key that unlocks every door in my life that You've ordained me to walk through? What is the key that I can take hold of, put in the door and turn so that it opens?"

This key has to do with the blood of Jesus. It comes through the bloodline. If I were to look at the DNA of Jesus Christ, I would find the DNA reveals the Father. I would find that Jesus is not the son of an earthly father, but He has the blood of the Deity. The blood running through His veins is not of bulls and goats. I'm talking about a blood with no impurities, no sin, no sickness, no HIV, no cancer, no migraines. A blood of purest form. Now that's the bloodline I want to tap into. If you're going to have a blood transfusion, you don't want blood donated by someone who has HIV or Leukemia. You want blood of the purest form.

If you're going to live in victory, if you're going to walk in the anointing, then you want to be tapped into the source of that bloodline—you want that same blood flowing through your veins. You want a cord going from heaven to you, connected to your veins into where that blood of purest form should be constantly flowing. So no matter where you are, you can expect victory every time. That blood has the power to call back your children into the household of God. That power can overcome every sickness. It has the power to protect you. It has the power to prosper you.

If there's anything the devil hates, it's the power that is within that bloodline. You see, he lived in heaven for a while. He knows scripture backward and forward more than you'll ever know it because he was there when it was created. He knows the power that is contained in the Word that speaks of the Blood! He is intimately familiar with that power—he knows that when you are covered in the blood there is a circle around you he cannot cross over. He knows the victory in that blood and it terrifies him.

Thank You Lord for Your sacrifice upon the cross. Thank You for pouring out Your Blood into my veins—the ultimate blood transfusion. For no other reason, I praise You today. You have caused my blood to run pure and holy, that I would be whole and worthy. Thank You for Your Life pulsing through my veins!

One Minute of Praise:

What does it mean to have the Blood of Christ circulating through you—spirit, soul *and body*? How does that affect your potential for overcoming the enemy? Think about the victory you could be walking in if you were able to take hold of this Truth in your heart through one minute of praise.

_____

_____

_____

_____

_____

_____

_____

_____

_____

EIGHT

The Power to Overcome

"Take special care of these lambs until the evening of the fourteenth day of this first month. Then each family in the community must slaughter its lamb. They are to take some of the lamb's blood and smear it on the top and sides of the doorframe of the house where the lamb will be eaten. That evening everyone must eat roast lamb with bitter herbs and bread made without yeast. The meat must never be eaten raw or boiled; roast it all.... Do not leave any of it until the next day. Whatever is not eaten that night must be burned before morning."

Exodus 12:6-10

One Minute of Praise

$\mathcal{T}$he power that is in the blood is the means for overcoming Satan. Do you see the instructions that God is giving the Israelites? There are conditions to God's promises, but they are always conditions that you can obey because He always prepares you before He requires your obedience to them.

Exodus 12:11 talks about such preparations: "Wear your traveling clothes as you eat this meal, as though prepared for a long journey. Wear your sandals and carry your walking stick." Say to yourself, "I am fixing to go on a journey." Look at your feet and see if you've got your Holy Ghost sandals on. Have you got a stick in your hand?

The passage goes on to say,

Eat the food quickly, for this is the Lord's Passover. On that night I will pass through the land of Egypt and kill all the firstborn sons and firstborn male animals in the land of Egypt. I will execute judgment against all the gods of Egypt, for I am the Lord! The blood you have smeared on your doorposts will serve as a sign. When I see the blood, I will pass over you. This plague of death will not touch you.

Exodus 12:11-13

When the blood is applied, the plague will not touch you. There is a power in the bloodline so when Satan comes near you, immediately he recognizes the anointing that rests upon you. The Word says to just speak the name of Jesus. You don't have to quote the whole book of Psalms. It just says speak the name of Jesus and Satan has to flee.

So after God gives all these instructions to the Israelites, He tells them, "After you've done all of this, I want you to go into your house and rest in peace." Now how many of you could go into your house, go to bed, get a good night's sleep when you know that tonight a death angel is coming through your neighborhood? It almost seems impossible, doesn't it? But if God said it then that means He is going to give them the peace they need to go inside and rest. Their faith was elevated to trust in what He'd promised. They went in to rest in peace because they did more than just believe and have faith. Their faith had been elevated to a trust because they knew who'd spoken the promise. In effect, they said, "I know! I know! I am confident because if God said it, I believe it, and that settles it."

Before the blood was applied to the doorpost, they lived in bondage. (They lived in houses of bondage.) But when the blood was applied to the doorpost, they became houses of faith. Is your house a house of bondage or a house of faith? As New Testament believers, we know that we are God's living temples of faith. We apply the blood by what we speak— the confessions that come forth from our mouth. What are you speaking? A blessing? Then you're applying the blood. A curse? Then you're removing the blood.

The New Living Translation says it this way: "Let the redeemed of the Lord say so." In other words, speak it

One Minute of Praise

out! "Has the Lord redeemed you? Then speak out!"
(Psalms 107:2)

Do you want to change your life? Then when you get up in the morning, give God one minute of praise. Don't ask Him for anything. Don't debate or discuss. Just worship Him. Put on your traveling clothes which prepares you for the day and your Holy Ghost sandals Who will direct your path. Then take up your walking stick that will give you supernatural power and begin to praise Him. Thank Him for what He has done for you. For one whole minute make it all about Him.

Praise you Lord for You are God! You are holy and worthy of praise! Mighty is Your name and how wonderful are Your works. Thank You for all the beauty and goodness You pour into my life and for Your never-ending grace and faithfulness. Thank You for Your love, Your truth, and Your endless mercy. I worship You and love you with all I am today.

One Minute of Praise:

What has the love of God meant to you?

_____

_____

_____

_____

III.

Divine Secrets of Praise

NINE

Praise Silences the Enemy

You have taught children and nursing infants to give you praise. They silence your enemies who were seeking revenge.

Psalm 8:2

I am going to equip you with a powerful weapon you will carry for the rest of your life. In Psalm 8:2, the Lord is saying, "I've taught the children and the nursing infants to give Me praise." And when they open their mouths to give Him praise, it says, "They silence your enemies who were seeking revenge." Wow! That's a powerful statement.

Praise Silences the Enemy

You might say to yourself, "Well, I haven't been saved very long. I don't have very much Word in me because I've been a Christian for a short time. That's just for the ultra-spiritual people." Not true! The Word says right here that even the infants—even the spiritual children—will open their mouths to praise God and silence their enemies. It makes no difference if you were saved last night, or if you've been saved for thirty years. It says when praise comes out of your mouth, you are silencing your enemy.

I like how the Russian Bible translates it—"When the saints of God praise God, the devil has no voice." Now if somebody has no voice, they can't speak. So therefore, the enemy cannot speak and put things in your mind because you have silenced him!

Do you want me to take you farther? Do you want to go deeper? Then look at Psalm 3:7 NASV: "You have smitten all my enemies on the cheek; You have shattered the teeth of the wicked." Think about it, when you get up in the morning and focus on praising God, even for one minute, not only are you going to silence your enemy, not only are you going to shut his mouth, but you are going to break his jaw-bone! Let me tell you, a person with a broken jawbone can't even whisper. They can't get a word out. This means the Lord is going to completely silence your enemy.

After He breaks the jawbone of your enemy, it says He's going to take away his identity. When somebody's corpse has been found and they cannot tell who it is, what is it that they look at to identify that person? Their teeth. So God will take the identity of something in your life—whether it's abuse, or sickness, or cancer, or leukemia, or a marriage situation, or unsaved kids, whatever is in your life—and destroy that mountain through the praise coming out of *your* mouth.

Praise is something He can work with. Praise gives Him something to inhabit in order to change a situation. When the blood has been applied, then God is going to take the enemy and not only silence him, but completely destroy all traces of his identity through your praise.

Hallelujah! Thank You Father for filling our mouths with praise, and filling our praise with your power! Stir our hearts, our minds and our tongues to speak forth praise and bring you glory every waking moment. Help us to recognize in our day of trouble that only through praising You will we overcome— remind us that the battle belongs to You, our Lord!

One Minute of Praise:

Is there a mountain looming in your life? Do you feel the enemy lurking? Take one minute right now to break his jawbone with your praise:

_____

_____

TEN

Turning Demons to Dust

You will be a new threshing instrument with many sharp teeth. You will tear all your enemies apart, making chaff of mountains. You will toss them in the air, and the wind will blow them all away; a whirlwind will scatter them. And the joy of the Lord will fill you to overflowing. You will glory in the Holy One of Israel.

Isaiah 41:15-16

When the Lord said, "You will tear all your enemies apart"—did He mean only some? Or only the ones that He wants to? Or just the easy ones? How many did He say? "You will tear *all* of my enemies apart, making chaff of mountains." Do you have a mountain in your life? Today it's going to be ground into powder!

Then it says He will toss them in the air. He's broken the jawbone. He's pulled all of the teeth out. He's ground them up and now they are powder. Now He's going to take any trace of the identity of your enemy—the one who has tried to destroy your life, your marriage, your job, your finances, or your health—and He's going to take that leftover powder and toss it into the air. And then it says in verse sixteen that a whirlwind will come and scatter it.

Now how far is He going to scatter it? Is He going to scatter it so that it can all come back and suddenly be there again? No, of course not! He is saying that He will take all of your iniquities, everything in the past, and cast it away as far as the east is from the west. Now I want to know how far is the east from the west? Because I want to know when I applied the blood is there a chance that my sins might come back and haunt me? Is there a chance that my sickness may come back? Is there a chance that my marriage might end up in a divorce?

When I praise God, Satan's jawbone is broken, his identity is ground, and ground, and ground beyond recognition—and then the Lord tosses the remaining dust into the air and the whirlwind blows it as far as the east is from the west—you won't be seeing that problem again.

Turning Demons to Dust

Through your praise, the Lord is going to take your enemy, He's going to take your sickness, He's going to take the problems in your family, and grind them into powder and toss them in the air. As He tosses that dust in the air, the wind of the Holy Spirit is going to come and take your need, your problem, your road block—and whatever the devil has tried to use to destroy your life—and He's going to scatter it as far as the east is from the west. All because you applied the blood to your life this morning—because you gave Him one minute of praise and didn't ask Him for anything. My goodness! Hallelujah! Can you think of a better reason to praise Him for one minute when you get out of bed in the morning?

Father God, I praise You with a grateful heart knowing You are worthy and almighty! Thank You for equipping me with the power to praise You with confidence and authority—making dust of enemies so that You can permanently scatter any trace on my behalf! Thank You for filling my praise with Your awesome Presence!

One Minute of Praise:

We all have more than an abundance of concerns, weaknesses, circumstances, and burdens. Take your focus off all of them and place your undivided attention on the answer—for one minute.

ELEVEN

Sharpen Your Sword

For the word of God is living and active, sharper than any two-edged sword, piercing to the division of soul and of spirit, of joints and of marrow, and discerning the thoughts and intentions of the heart.

Hebrews 4:12 ESV

The Lord tells us that He has equipped us with a double-edged sword. We want it sharp on both sides—because if we don't keep our sword sharpened, it becomes dull and won't even cut a piece of paper. "But how do I keep my sword sharpened?" you might ask. To sharpen your sword, you use the Word like a whetstone. When you put the Word in your heart, it polishes one side. You see, you can't speak out to the enemy if you have nothing in you to speak out.

Some of you are trying to get by on what you learned in Sunday school—but you've got to get a fresh word, a new word, a revelation of what God has to say to you *today*.

Sometimes, when I'm sitting at a red light, I read my scripture cards. All they have written on them is one verse of scripture so I can pick up a scripture and read it anytime, anywhere. For instance, one card I have says, "Greater is He that is in you, than He that is in the world." (1 John 4:4 KJV) I look at my scripture cards when I'm washing dishes, or waiting on my husband to go somewhere. I have my cards near me or I have my Bible open almost all of the time so that I can put His Word into me. Then when a situation comes that threatens myself or my family, I begin to speak the Word out, and polish the other edge of my sword—"God, you said you'd be closer to me than a brother. You said You would never leave me or forsake me"— You polish one side of your weapon as the Word goes in and then the other side as the Word comes out.

You are equipped with a two-edged sword that will destroy your enemy. You can totally annihilate him because your sword has been sharpened to divide the dark from the light. You can cut the bad the devil has for you away from the good God has intended for you. Yet too many are trying to destroy the enemy with dull weapons, and they can't figure out why their swords aren't more effective.

Let me tell you a story to illustrate this. It's about a lady in her nineties. She loved God with all her heart. She went regularly to intercessory prayer at her church. She had been faithfully interceding—praying and praying and praying. One night on her way home, she was just so in love with God. She spoke out the Word, was praying in tongues, and having a wonderful time. When she arrived home, she noticed her door was ajar. She thought, *Now, I didn't leave that door open.* So she walked in and caught a burglar red-handed in her house stealing her possessions. It made her mad. Here she was at church praying and interceding with her face on the carpet, and while she was there the devil was at her house trying to steal her goods. *I ain't going to put up with it!* she told herself.

So she points her little, old lady finger at the robber and said, "Acts 2:38! Repent of your sins!" He froze. He couldn't move. He was paralyzed and trembling. Then she said, "You stay right there. I'm going to call 911." When the police got there, he still hadn't moved. They couldn't understand it. There was this little, old, close to a hundred-year-old woman, all withered up, and without an ounce of strength, and there is this young, robust robber standing there scared out of his wits. He could have taken her out with one blow, but he had not moved. Now she was just walking around like there wasn't a problem. The policeman asked, "What did you say to him?"

She said, "Acts 2:38. Repent of your sins."

They walked over to the thief and asked, "Do you know what she said to you?"

"Yes, sir. I do."

The policeman said, "She quoted you a scripture."

He said, "Are you kidding me? That old woman told me she had an axe and two .38s and I wasn't about to move!"

Now let me tell you what your one minute of praise will do. Your one minute of praise this morning equips you with an axe and two .38s. So no matter where you go, if you've given Him praise and you've applied the Blood to your life—even though no one can see it—you have pulled out your axe and two .38s and the enemy will be totally stunned.

Hallelujah! Praise You Father God for equipping me with a two-edge sword! Help me to keep it sharp by daily meditating on Your Word and speaking it forth. Remind me to make the most of every opportunity to stun my enemies with Your praises!

One Minute of Praise:

What can you do right now to sharpen your sword? Whatever Word is in your heart, take one minute to speak it out now—and begin sharpening away!

_____

_____

_____

TWELVE

Target Your Praise

Do not fret or have any anxiety about anything, but in every circumstance and in everything, by prayer and petition (definite requests), with thanksgiving, continue to make your wants known to God.

Philippians 4:6 AMP

Perhaps you aren't getting the desire of your heart because you have only been praying surface prayers. Surface prayers do not move God—He wants you to speak to the root. What is keeping your husband from living for God? Is it alcohol? Is it drugs? Is it another woman? Is it low self-esteem? What is causing the children in your home to rebel? Is it the friends they hang around? Is it the music they listen to or the television they watch? When you're at work, why is it that your boss doesn't treat you fairly? Is it because of jealousy? Or is it because he doesn't like you being a Christian?

If you want your husband delivered from alcohol, then you need to begin speaking and taking authority over alcoholism. Don't just say, "Lord, I want you to save my husband." You must destroy the root of this problem. If you go in your front yard and there's a weed growing, and you walk over and break the top off, in two or three days that weed will come back. But if you go deeper into the ground and pull it up by the root, it won't be back the next day, or the next, or the next, because you have completely removed it up by removing the root. The weed is gone and won't bother you again.

Start praying for the root of what's in your household. Stop praying for the salvation of your husband. Stop praying for the salvation of your kids. "I don't understand," you're saying. "My husband and children need to be saved." Ask yourself instead, "What is in my husband's life that isn't Christian-like?" Is it pornography? Then that's the root. Start praying against pornography. Start praying against drugs. Take authority over alcohol. Take authority over a foul mouth. Take authority over lying. Get specific. You've got to target your prayer. If you don't, you're just stunning the enemy. If you don't get anything up by the root, it grows back. You see, when you pray for salvation, you're just praying over the fruit. You've got to get to the root because it takes more than just a surface prayer.

I'm not saying, "Don't pray for the salvation." You've simply got to go beyond praying general prayers. You've got to be more specific. You've got to go for the bull's eyes, not the circles around the bull's eye.

You've been praying to God with tears coursing down your face, but now it's time to target those prayers. Make it clear to Satan exactly what you are taking authority over. Say something like, "I am praying against the drugs," or "I am praying for my finances," or "I am speaking purity over my children who are abusing me verbally." Target your prayers like a sharp shooter. You will begin to see the answers appear because you've focused in on the bull's eyes.

Some of you have been shooting around the target and you've missed the whole board. Instead you need to be specific, accurate, and precise. Don't waste your energy—or your words—on mindless surface prayers. Pray to understand what the root of the issue is, pray for discernment, and then take authority with precision.

Father God, help me expand my focus beyond symptoms and to narrow in on root causes so I can pray effectively. I thank You for your wisdom and divine insight into my situation—I thank You for Your Holy Spirit and the mind of Christ. Help me to make the most of my prayers and words of praise.

Target Your Praise

One Minute of Praise:

Think for a moment about your concerns. What might be some of the root issues that you haven't considered before? Praise God for addressing those specific areas—for one minute:

_____

_____

_____

_____

_____

_____

_____

_____

THIRTEEN

Why We Praise Him

But He was wounded for our transgressions, He was bruised for our iniquities; The chastisement for our peace was upon Him, And by His stripes we are healed.

Isaiah 53:5 NKJV

*H*ave you seen the movie *The Passion of the Christ?* My worship totally changed after I saw this depiction of Jesus' Crucifixion. Suddenly I could see what I was worshipping. I could imagine it before, but now I saw it. The blood we saw dripping from His body in that movie represented the blood shed by the Son of God because our Heavenly Father said, "I want to give My people authority. I want to give them superpower. I want to empower them to walk confidently every single day of their life. So I will send My Son as a sacrifice so they can have all things pertaining to life and godliness."

We have heard so much about "by Your stripes we are healed"—but I'm not sure we really appreciate the depth or full meaning of those stripes. Do you realize that Jesus bled from five distinct areas on His body? The first was from his head as the crown of thorns was placed on his brow. As those thorns bit into His skull and blood began to course down His face, Jesus knew there would be someone with mental issues His blood would provide healing for—or emotional hurts His blood could bind. He knew there would be someone with migraine headaches who needed healing—someone emotionally unstable or who goes to bed at night falling victim to nightmare after nightmare—and He knew this blood was ordained for their healing. By the shedding of that blood He could remove bitterness, unforgiveness, or anything else that tried to take over their mind with its bondage.

The second area He bled from was His back. Beaten until almost unrecognizable, Jesus bore a stripe to provide healing for any sickness that would ever come into your life. The price was paid. He bore a stripe for cancer, a stripe for leukemia, a stripe for headaches, sore throats, broken bones, and crippled feet. The blood that coursed down His back promised healing to any who wanted to receive.

As His hands took the nails that fastened them to the cross, they also bled. The anguish and pain He suffered as they drove each nail into His hands said: "I have shed this blood because the Word says to lay hands on the sick and they shall recover." So by the piercing of His hands, your hands have been anointed to heal the sick. This blood was also shed so that everything you lay your hand to would prosper.

Then nails were driven into His feet. Why did He have to shed blood from His feet? So that your steps could be ordered by the Lord. So that everyday when you get up and praise comes out of your mouth, your steps will be ordered of God. You don't have to see every step from where you are now to where you're going; all you need to see is the next step. Some of you are going to walk through territory you've never been in before—territory that might frighten you if you knew where God was taking you—but you're going to take the Word as a roadmap to conquer that territory step by step because God is guiding you.

As Jesus hung on the cross between heaven and hell, it says that the anguish was so severe that God had to turn His face from His beloved Son. He could not look upon Him as He hung there alone. At this, Jesus cried out, "*Eli, Eli, lama sabachthanai?*" that is, "My God, My God, why have You forsaken Me?" (see Matthew 27:46 NKJV.) And with his last breath he uttered, "Into Thy hands I commit My spirit."

 Why We Praise Him

But there was still one more healing that had not transpired, because He knew there would be someone suffering from a broken heart. I'm not talking about a broken heart from a relationship, but the broken heart that comes from a way of life. It is the broken heart of those who have given up hope. It is the broken heart of a woman who feels that every wife must be abused, or a man living from paycheck to paycheck struggling to provide food for his family—the deep wounds of those who feel there is no escape, no other options, who walk around with a heart perpetually aching from life's disappointments, convinced they should never expect any better.

When the Roman soldier came and looked at Jesus Christ who had already given up His spirit to God, he took his spear and thrust it into the side of Jesus. When he did, the tip of it pierced the heart, and out flowed blood and water from a broken heart. Psalms 147:3 tells us, "He heals the brokenhearted." This blood too was shed for you.

Oh Lord, my Savior, You have provided for my health spirit, soul, and body. I receive your precious gift of healing from the top of my head to the tips of my toes. I put my trust in the blood of Christ for soundness of mind, wholeness of body, grace upon my hands, and for directing my steps—but most importantly, for restoring my heart. Thank You Lord Jesus for providing all of this by shedding Your blood upon the cross for me.

One Minute of Praise:

Where do you need restoration? By the blood of Jesus and the word of your testimony you shall overcome. What is the word of your testimony? Write it down now:

_____

_____

_____

_____

_____

_____

_____

_____

IV.

The Purpose of Praise

FOURTEEN

A Throne of Sweet Fragrance

Yet you are holy, enthroned on the praises of Israel. In you our fathers trusted; they trusted, and you delivered them.

Psalm 22:3,4 ESV

Life comes crashing down. You lost your job. Your marriage of forty years has ended. Your child was killed in a car accident last year. You were just told you have breast cancer. What do you do? Why go on?

You wonder, "Is life really a gift?" You seem to lack the strength to get up in the morning. You've stopped having conversations with your friends. You hide in seclusion. Your heart is smashed into a million pieces. You find yourself imprisoned in your own self-pity. You have no clue where to turn. The future seems so dark and dim. In times of trouble where do you go?

How did David find victory? Where did David go in his many times of despair?

David says in Psalms 22:3 that God is enthroned on the praises of His people. David knew he could create a place for God to come down and sit with him during his valley experiences and his mountain victories. Every King has a throne to sit on and from that throne he rules his kingdom. Your praise prepares a place for the King of Kings to sit and rule in your life. Your praise builds a throne in the heavenlies from which He reigns. Your praise clears out a territorial position in the atmosphere from which He comes and rules. The enemy has no authority over you because you are no longer ruling; your Heavenly Father has taken position and now sits on the throne that you have created for Him and rules over your adversary. He controls the enemy that desires to bring harm to you. He speaks healing to your broken heart. He brings peace to a mind that is on the verge of a nervous breakdown. He puts a marriage back together. Your praise becomes a sweet aroma to His nostrils and He just cannot stay away.

Have you noticed how important this fragrance is to God? The sins of the Israelites were often described as a stench in the nostrils of God. Esther's preparation for the King was a part of the key to her receiving his favor. She bathed in special oils that gave her a pleasing scent. Wise men gave frankincense and myrrh to the Christ Child as a gift. Mary broke an alabaster box of fragrant oil to anoint the feet of Jesus and sweet aroma filled the room. In the same way, you can send up a sweet-smelling savor to God; a scent that He is so attracted to, that you become irresistible to Him.

In the Old Testament the Israelites communed with God through the Altar of Incense. In Exodus 30:22-38, God gave detailed instructions for making a special blend of oil and incense that was never to be used for anything besides the Tabernacle worship. Oil and incense were set apart for worship only. The symbolic importance of this composition was twofold. The first was to draw the favor of God by the pleasant smell—to make Him more willing to hear the petitions that were going to be made to Him. If the offering was accepted, it was called a sweet savor—if not, it was called a "stinking savor." The other symbolic use was represented by the dense cloud of smoke that made for a kind of covering to hide the sins of the people from the face of God.[1]

Thus the fragrance of the holy oil and incense, as it was used in the service of the Tabernacle, was to be unique and unmistakable, a reminder to the people, with every breath they had of it, that God was in their midst.

 A Throne of Sweet Fragrance

Your praise when given unto the Lord has a fragrance just like the holy oil and incense used in the Tabernacle. It becomes a unique and unmistakable reminder that you have invited God to be in your midst with every breath of praise you offer.

As David did, and the fathers of old, help me to enthrone You in my praises. Make them a sweet smelling sacrifice that is pleasing to You. Give me a deeper revelation of how sweet my songs of praise are to You, and how powerful and wonderful is Your presence that resides in their midst.

One Minute of Praise:

Be conscious of the Lord. Offer up a sweet fragrance to woo Him into your midst, and then as if building a throne for the Lord to come and rest upon, continue to lift up your praises:

_____

_____

_____

_____

_____

_____

FIFTEEN

The Fall before the Fall

You were the seal of perfection, Full of wisdom and perfect in beauty. You were in Eden, the garden of God; Every precious stone was your covering: The sardius, topaz, and diamond, Beryl, onyx, and jasper, Sapphire, turquoise, and emerald with gold. The workmanship of your timbrels and pipes Was prepared for you on the day you were created. You were the anointed cherub who covers; I established you; You were on the holy mountain of God; You walked back and forth in the midst of fiery stones.

You were perfect in your ways from the day you were created, Till iniquity was found in you.

Ezekiel 28:12-15 NKJV

*P*raise was introduced into heaven long before we were placed upon this earth. God created Lucifer, the most beautiful angel in heaven, and placed him in charge of heaven's orchestra.

The Hebrew word for timbrels found in Ezekiel 28:13 is *toph* which comes from *taphaph* (taw-faf), which means "to drum or to play like a tambourine." You also find the word *pipes* in that same verse which had the sound of a wind instrument such as a flute.

There was music outwardly, but also a sound that came from within—every time Lucifer breathed, he would produce a song that was tied into praise.

As he breathed and moved through Heaven—he called and the angelic beings were ushered into worship. In unison they begin to sing, Holy, Holy, Holy, "Thou art worthy, O Lord, to receive glory and honour and power: for thou hast created all things, and for thy pleasure they are and were created." (Revelation 4:11 KJV)

Lucifer was more beautiful than any other being in Heaven. In Ezekiel 28:15 we read that he was perfect in all his ways from the day he was created. But the last part of that verse says, "'til iniquity was found in you."

Lucifer's power over all the angels in Heaven caused him to elevate his own self worth. He convinced himself that he could take the place of God. He began to tell himself how beautiful and powerful he was in comparison with all the other heavenly beings. A third of the angels began to brag on him and encourage him to overtake the Kingdom. They were so convincing that he began to believe it was possible. He forgot who had created him in the beginning. He dismissed any thought that without God he would not exist.

Be careful when everything seems to be spiraling upward as if nothing could go wrong. There's money in the bank, you've moved into a new house, and you have two Mercedes in the garage for you and your lovely wife. Your kids are getting a good education and you're up for a promotion next week. Remember from where you came. Let's not forget who gave you breath and the strength to work. Satan will tempt you with a small voice saying, "Why do you need God right now? Look where you have come from and how hard you have worked to get where you are. You deserve a day at the lake with the family. I know it's Sunday, but He'll understand this once. You've put in a lot of hours, you deserve some time away with your family." Before long, you find yourself only going to church on Easter, Mother's Day, and Christmas.

What happened? Pride set in. You thought you were able to control everything around you and that your success was within your own power to dictate. But one day,

The Fall before the Fall 63

unexpectedly, your world falls apart. You have a massive heart attack, work goes on hold, and you find yourself in bankruptcy.

I believe in the blessings of God. I know that God can bless financially and physically. But I also believe to continue to walk in the blessings of God, He must continually be honored and respected.

Lord, help me not to take your blessings for granted. Make me mindful every moment of Your divine grace and favor that causes me to succeed in every area of life. Help me to trust only in You, and not in my own strength or the power of others. You alone are worthy of all praise and honor.

One Minute of Praise:

Don't neglect giving honor where it is due. Take one minute to glorify the Lord:

_____

_____

_____

_____

_____

_____

SIXTEEN

A New Age of Praise

O my Strength, I will sing praises to you, for you, O God, are my fortress, the God who shows me steadfast love.

Psalm 59:17 ESV

Isaiah 14:13 shares with us how Lucifer said he would ascend into heaven and set his throne above God. He would climb to the highest heavens and be like the Most High. But God replied, "You will be brought down to the place of the dead, down to its lowest depths." (Isaiah 14:15) After pride consumed Lucifer, we find in Revelations 12 that

God removed one third of the angels along with Lucifer from Heaven—and so began the war against God.

Lucifer's role of orchestrating Heaven's worship had ended. But God had a plan to return worship to Heaven. He said, "I will make man and I will create him in my image. I will breathe celestial air into his nostrils and he will become a living soul, created to praise and worship me." So with his tender but powerful anointed hands, he created man. Man became a living soul. What a joy it was for God to have Adam and Eve to walk with in the cool of the evening. Wouldn't you like to have been there to hear their conversation? What would God, the ruler of the Universe, and Adam and Eve, created in perfection, talk about? What ever it was, they were having an awesome time.

Satan was angry—angry with God, and angry with man. Man had become a worshipper of the One who had created him and they had become best friends. When man was created in the Garden of Eden, Satan was determined to drive a wedge between God and man. So by convincing Eve to eat of the forbidden fruit he did just that.

Satan thought he had won, but realized on Easter Sunday that God still rules—God still had authority over him. God was still in control and Satan could not stop what God had started. Man would continue to fulfill the destiny God ordained for him—to give God praise forever.

One Minute of Praise

Lucifer understands the power in praise. He will do everything possible to distract you from the One who gives you daily strength, power, and wisdom. He will try to convince you that you can make it okay by yourself. It's a slow, subtle process—but he will attempt to cause you to justify every action you take to leave God out of your life. Let's be reminded of the One who gives us breath to live—and removes our breath when He decides it is time for us to cease living.

Psalms 139 tells us how well God knows us, is ever with us, and is all seeing, all knowing, all-powerful, and ever-present.

O Lord, You have searched me and known me. You know my sitting down and my rising up; You understand my thought afar off. You comprehend my path and my lying down, And are acquainted with all my ways. For there is not a word on my tongue, But behold, O Lord, You know it altogether. You have hedged me behind and before, And laid Your hand upon me. Such knowledge is too wonderful for me; It is high, I cannot attain it. Where can I go from Your Spirit? Or where can I flee from Your presence? If I ascend into heaven, You are there; If I make my bed in hell, behold, You are there. If I take the wings of the morning, And dwell in the uttermost parts of the sea, Even there

A New Age of Praise

Your hand shall lead me, And Your right hand shall hold me. If I say, "Surely the darkness shall fall on me," Even the night shall be light about me; Indeed, the darkness shall not hide from You, But the night shines as the day; The darkness and the light are both alike to You. For You formed my inward parts; You covered me in my mother's womb. I will praise You, for I am fearfully and wonderfully made; Marvelous are Your works, And that my soul knows very well.

Psalm 139:1-14 NKJV

No wonder Satan wants to steal your praise. Listen to what God says about you; you mean everything to Him! Don't be tricked by the devil into thinking any other way. Throughout the ages of time, God has spent a lot of energy thinking about you. Before He ever created you He knew you were going to make mistakes, mess up, have shortcomings, and hit a few bumps in the road. And He still created you exactly as you are.

What do you do when life comes crashing down and you are imprisoned in the tomb of your own self-pity? You choose to shout to the mountaintop as David did in Psalms 59:16 : "But as for me, I will sing about your power. I will shout with joy each morning because of your unfailing love. For you have been my refuge; a place of safety in the day of distress."

Thank you Lord for loving me where I am, and for never leaving or forsaking me. I am your workmanship, a worshipper, created to bring you praise—a vessel of honor prepared to bring you glory. Thank you for completing the good work you have begun in me.

One Minute of Praise:

Your destiny is to bring praise and glory to God. Don't let the rocks cry out on your behalf, don't let the enemy keep you from creating an atmosphere of praise. Bring heaven to earth on the expressway of your praise for the next sixty seconds:

SEVENTEEN

Let the Redeemed Say So

Let the redeemed of the LORD say so, Whom He has redeemed from the hand of the enemy.

Psalm 107:2 NKJV

*W*e've learned how Lucifer was the director of worship in heaven. He was the director of music. When Lucifer opened his mouth, the pipes and organs would resonate through heaven and the timbrels around him would begin to sound, he would literally call heaven into worship. And the angelic host would all begin to bow down and cry out to God, "Holy, holy, holy."

One Minute of Praise

But then pride set in and he was kicked out of heaven along with one third of the angels. God longed for worship to be restored to heaven so He said, "I'll create a man. I will create a being that will worship Me here from earth."

So we know the story of how He created Adam and Eve. One thing I like about the creation story is how everything that the Lord created He spoke it into existence. He said, "Let there be light," and there was light. He spoke and the water and the land separated. But when it came to man, when it came to the creation that He was going to form in His own image, He created this with His hands. That's something very precious. He didn't just say, "Let there be Adam," and there he was. But He said, "I've got to create something that I can breathe My life into and make into My image."

So if I were to ask you today, "What do you think about God?" You'd say, "He's pretty awesome!" Well, if you were created in His image then what does that make you? You are just as awesome—fearfully and wonderfully made by the hands of the Creator Himself! Never allow anyone to tell you otherwise. If you were created in His image, then you were created to be something awesome. And with His power and the Holy Ghost residing in you, there is nothing you can't do if your mind can conceive it.

Then Satan came into the Garden of Eden. He came in and drove a wedge between man and God. Before that, the Father would come down and walk alongside Adam and Eve every single day. Once again God said, "I have someone that can enjoy and worship My Glory—someone I can commune with." Satan hated Adam. He despised him because he now had fellowship with God. If Satan no longer has fellowship with God, satan is determined that man won't either.

But I have news for the devil today. The Word says when we get to heaven; the angels will have to step aside because they will be stunned silent for thirty minutes. We will be singing a song that the angels have never even sung—and I think it'll go something like this.

Redeemed how I love to proclaim it.

Redeemed by the blood of the Lamb.

Redeemed through His infinite mercy.

His child and forever I am.

Redeemed, redeemed, redeemed by the blood of the Lamb.

Redeemed, redeemed, redeemed; His child and forever I am.

And do you know why we'll be able to sing that song? Because we have been bought for a price. Satan was never bought for a price. The angels have not been bought for a price. But we, the creation made in the image of God, have been bought for a price. I believe when we get to heaven and we begin to sing that song, *Redeemed, Redeemed by the Blood*, the angel's are going to say, "We've been hearing a lot of worship coming from the earth below for many, many years. We've been standing here as the worship has come up and the songs have been sung." But the angels are going to say, "But wait a minute. We've never heard this one before. We've got to step aside. This is a new song." Then God began to say, "Come on, children of mine. Come with me." And God is going to take us to the throne right beside Him—the place that Lucifer was created to be but will not be. That's where God is going to usher us—directly beside Him. Man, who was created lower than the angels, one day will be higher, will be elevated higher than the host of angelic beings in heaven, and will sit on the throne beside God—forever, and forever, and forever. Hallelujah.

God is looking for people who will radiate His glory and hunger for His presence.

You, Oh Lord, are faithful to meet us right where we worship You—to commune with us as we lift our voices and declare Your praises. We lift up holy hands and are humbled and honored to lead the heavens in a new song of worshipful praise. Let the saints be glad and the redeemed declare that the Lord reigns forever!

Let the Redeemed Say So

One Minute of Praise:

Lift up a new song! Rejoice for you are made in His image and ordained to lead the heavens in worship forevermore!

_____

_____

_____

_____

_____

_____

_____

_____

V.

The Keepers of His Praise

EIGHTEEN

Created for Praise

Then she knelt behind him at his feet, weeping. Her tears fell on his feet, and she wiped them off with her hair. Then she kept kissing his feet and putting perfume on them.

Luke 7:38

ack in the day of Jesus, it was customary when someone went to a house to visit, the servants would meet them at the front door. As they entered, they would take their sandals off and wash their feet. The servants would then bring them in and anoint them with oil. It was just as common as when we wash our hands before we sit down to eat.

In Luke chapter seven, we find that Jesus has walked all day long. Unless you were wealthy and owned a donkey or a horse, you walked everywhere you traveled. So after a day of walking, Jesus must have been very hot and sweaty, and probably covered in dust. He arrives at this house and they treat Him like one of the boys—they showed no honor or respect to Him.

But here we find Mary fallen at His feet. The Bible calls her a sinful woman. She looked up into His face and said, "Lord, you've changed my whole life." It brought tears of gratitude that flowed down her cheeks. And then as the tears fell on his feet, she began to wipe them off. She took the one thing that was most glorious to her, her hair, and begins to wipe off all the sand, dirt, and mud from His feet. Finally, she took the next most precious thing, worth a whole year of wages, an entire bottle of precious perfume, and poured it out upon His feet.

Now let's move over to Luke chapter ten. We find Mary, the sister of Martha and Lazarus. And the Lord said to Martha, "My dear Martha, you are so upset over all of these details! There is really only one thing worth being concerned about. Mary has discovered it—and I won't take it away from her" (Luke 10:41-42).

What Mary the sister of Martha had discovered was something that the others had not. Mary had learned what it was like to go from one glory, to another glory, to another glory. Jesus said that once you have been in the presence of the Lord God Almighty, once you have been there, He would not take that away from you because He knows how precious that is to you. He said, "Don't you understand? This is what I created her for. I created her to come and kneel before Me. I created her tears to roll down and fall at My feet, because My feet are the most precious part of Me. She's only doing what I created her to do—and that is to worship Me."

Satan may have taken worship out of heaven. He may have driven it out of the Garden of Eden. But I stand here today and proclaim that he will not take it out of the hearts of men. In John 12:3 we again read about Mary: "Then Mary took a twelve-ounce jar of expensive perfume made from essence of nard, and she anointed Jesus' feet with it and wiped his feet with her hair. And the house was filled with fragrance."

Now this was not long after Jesus raised Lazarus from the dead and was invited over to dinner at Lazarus' house. Lazarus was there, Martha was there, and Judas was there. And this is where we find Mary sitting at His feet. She is pouring this expensive perfume out on His feet. Judas goes to Jesus and says, "What a waste of money. She could have given this to the poor. What a waste of money." Judas is talking face to face with Jesus, who knows everything about Judas, who has been dipping into the bucket of the disciples' money for years. I believe when the eyes of Jesus met the eyes of Judas, he just shriveled up and scampered away. We don't read that he said anything else, do we?

So what does Jesus say to Judas? "Leave her alone." I think that's all He had to say. I think sometimes the Lord looks down on us when we're going, "Na, na, na, na, na, na

One Minute of Praise

about someone." He's saying, "Leave them alone. Back off and leave them alone. They're My creation. Who gives you authority to pass judgment over them?" The Word says, "bless and curse not." If you speak a curse out, what have you just done to yourself?

Now Simon called this sinful woman a sinner. Martha called her sister Mary lazy and Judas called her wasteful. But I think God called her precious. God is looking for people to pursue Him as these two Marys did. If you will only learn how to chase Him, to continually long for His Presence, you will find Him. You will find Him because He longs to be with You. When you chase Him, you will find yourself face to face with Him—and that's when intimacy begins between you and the heavenly Father.

Lord, today I will pursue only You. I will put away worrying and striving and simply sit at Your feet. Help me to be more like Mary—to take the best the world has to give and offer it to You. All You require of me is to rest and bask in Your Presence. Help me to do this one, simple thing for You in this moment now.

One Minute of Praise:

Rest in the Lord. Be still, rest, and sit before Him. Pour the sweet fragrance of your praise out over His beautiful feet—for just one minute:

Created for Praise

NINETEEN

A Passion for His Presence

For we are the temple of the living God; as God said, I will make my dwelling among them and walk among them, and I will be their God, and they shall be my people.

2 Corinthians 6:16 ESV

When God speaks about David's tabernacle, He calls it His "favorite house." In the Old Testament He writes about coming back to rebuild David's tabernacle. Why is He going to return and rebuild that particular tabernacle? Why not Solomon's temple? Why not Moses' tabernacle?

One Minute of Praise

First of all, in David's tabernacle there was no veil. Basically, it was a piece of tarp with a few sticks. I believe that is one reason God said, "I'm going to come back and rebuild it. It won't just be man-made—because man-made tabernacles deteriorate. But the temple I build will not deteriorate because it will be built within the soul."

So here we find David's tabernacle. It had no veil on the inside, and on the outside it was surrounded by worshippers and praisers. They just didn't worship Him on Sunday morning or Wednesday night. They praised God seven days a week, twenty-four hours a day, fifty-two weeks out of the year, three-hundred and sixty-five days a year. Every day was filled with praise and worship. And as the worship went up, I believe the Lord stood up and said, "Hold on a minute. I'm being summoned. My presence must go to them because their worship is drawing Me like a magnet. Their worship is calling Me."

What would happen in our congregations if we worshipped God until His presence overcame us? Because it's His presence that brings healing, comforts us, restores relationships and brings peace to every area of our lives. But until His presence consumes us, we remain unchanged.

David's passion for God did not start when he decided to bring the Ark of the Covenant back to Jerusalem. It started in the field where he sat out as a shepherd boy. He would sit all alone with his sheep and a harp. He would strum that harp and sing God's praises. I believe that as he worshiped,

A Passion for His Presence 81

the presence of God would come upon him wherever he was. He was never alone because the presence of God was with him. He learned as a child what it was like to enter into worship and for God to come down and consume him.

But see, passion doesn't start after you have arrived at a certain destination in life. You can't wait until you get behind the pulpit to become passionate. Passion doesn't suddenly appear after you get a title and a position. You get a passion when the servant's towel is handed to you and you say, "No matter, God. Wherever You want me. Whatever You want, I will serve You. If it's taking care of the sheep out in the back forty, I will serve You. And I will worship You." And the presence of God will come down and enable you to reorder your steps to walk up higher.

David had a passion for God. As he grew older he began to talk about bringing back the Ark of the Covenant. He wasn't interested in this beautiful box—he was consumed by the blue flame that resided within. Do you remember what the blue flame stood for? The presence of God. He said, "I've got to bring the presence of God back to Jerusalem."

God did not choose to rebuild Moses' temple, nor Solomon's temple. He said, "It's David's temple that I want. I want My presence available to man twenty-four hours a day." The blue flame goes with you no matter where you are.

In the New Testament, what happened at the crucifixion when the veil was ripped from top to bottom? Who became that temple? You did. You are now that temple. When He said He was going to rebuild His temple, He was talking about coming to reside in you. He is going to rebuild that passion that David had in every single one of us.

Praise You Lord for Your breathtaking plan! The thought that You would come to dwell in me takes my breathe away. Thank You for making me Your living temple in this earth. Thank You for filling me with Your Presence as I praise You today. Holy Spirit, help to make me into the sort of temple that God would want to inhabit as I offer myself a living sacrifice through my praises to Him. Help me to be a vessel of glory and honor prepared for every good work. Amen.

One Minute of Praise:

As a temple of the Living God, invite Him to make Himself at home in you for the next sixty seconds.

TWENTY

Humble, Holy, and Hungry

Do you not know that you are God's temple and that God's Spirit dwells in you? ...For God's temple is holy, and you are that temple.

1 Corinthians 3:16,17 ESV

How can we house the glory of God? First of all, we must have a humble spirit. Second, we must have a holy life. As Paul said, "I have to die daily." We never arrive at the point we don't need to repent. As long as Satan is alive, he's going to tempt, and he's going to fight, and he's going to try to destroy. So it's a daily dying.

The third thing is hungry. We must be hungry for the presence of God. If you are not hungry, then you are not going to long for it. If you've just eaten a big meal and somebody invites you over, it makes no difference what they have on their table—if you're not hungry, it's won't be appetizing to you. But when you are hungry, when you've gone all day without eating and you're starving, then the simplest fare looks delicious. God is looking for a group of people that are so hungry that they savor every precious moment of His Presence. And when they do, it shows everywhere they go, and with everyone they meet.

Housing the glory of God must begin in your own home. Your home should be the first sanctuary you dedicate to the Lord and the first place you practice walking in His Presence. By staying humble, holy, and hungry for more of God, you create an atmosphere in your home where the Spirit can reside affecting everyone who lives there.

You might find yourself dusting after your husband has gone to work, after the kids are off to school, and you come across that stack of dirty dishes in the sink and the piles of dirty laundry on the floor. You go through the motions of picking up after everyone, cleaning up all the messes they've left behind, and you're thinking, "Man, these people are a bunch of pigs." You go by the kids' rooms and you are tempted to put up a sign that says, "Caution. Needs fumigating." And then it all begins to well up inside of you. You go into your bedroom and there are his shoes, his

 Humble, Holy, and Hungry

socks, his tie, and you think, "Could he not walk four feet to the closet?" Then there's the shower towel and there's the underwear and you think, "Could he not at least have put his underwear in the dirty clothes? Why does he leave it out there for the whole house to see?"

Women, let me tell you something. It's an honor to pick up those socks. It's an honor to pick up that underwear because if you don't there will be some woman who wishes she could be there to do it instead. The thing is, you are a gift to him. Your husband, believe it or not, is a gift to you as well. So you have a choice. You can get bent out of shape—get so upset by the end of the day that you lose it as soon as your husband comes home from work and asks, "Hey honey, what's for supper?" just before he plops down on the sofa and yells, "Where's the remote control?" Or you can choose to be grateful.

You may find your mouth shouting out, "Remote control? What do you mean remote control? Do you know what I've been doing around here all day?"—As he turns to look at you with an expression that says, "Well, what happened to you?"

That's when you know you are not walking in humility, holiness, or hungering for more of God. What do you do? You stop and thank God you have a house to clean. You could be living beneath a bridge. You thank the Lord that you have a husband because you could be a single parent or living all alone. Suddenly, you'll find your gratitude is dispelling that self-righteousness, and you answer softly. You go about your chores singing and dancing. The Lord has become your strength and the next thing you know your husband is thinking, "Whoa, Baby! It's so good to see you!" And he's asking himself, "What's happened? This woman's on drugs! She must have had an antihistamine today," when all it is, is the joy of the Lord in your heart.

You have a choice. You can house the glory of God through your attitudes and behaviors, changing atmospheres and circumstances, even other people's hearts, or grieve His Spirit so that He will be found nowhere near you or your home.

Thank you Father God for making me mindful of my attitudes before they turn into words and behaviors that I will regret. Help me to keep an attitude of gratitude and walk humbly, holy, and ever more hungry for Your Presence.

Humble, Holy, and Hungry

One Minute of Praise:

Think about a situation, or a person, that is especially annoying to you at present. What can you think of around that particular issue to be grateful for? Direct those thoughts to the Lord—let go of your tendency to justify your feelings—leave out all the "buts" and "why for's"—for one whole minute, simply express your gratitude.

_____

_____

_____

_____

_____

_____

_____

_____

_____

TWENTY-ONE

The Glory Within

Remember, dear brothers and sisters, that few of you were wise in the world's eyes, or powerful, or wealthy when God called you. Instead, God deliberately chose things the world considers foolish in order to shame those who think they are wise. And he chose those who are powerless to shame those who are powerful. God chose things despised by the world, things counted as nothing at all, and used them to bring to nothing what the world considers important, so that no one can ever boast in the presence of God. God alone made it possible for you to be in Christ Jesus. For our benefit God made Christ to be wisdom itself. He is the one who made us acceptable to God. He made us pure and holy, *and he gave himself to purchase our freedom. As the Scriptures say, "The person who wishes to boast should boast only of what the Lord has done."*

1 Corinthians 1:26-31

God is saying here that He needs people that have no power within themselves. God knows that if He chose someone that has no power within him- or herself—that doesn't know how to do what needs to be done—he or she will totally rely on Him. That's what the Lord is saying here, "If you boast you boast unto Me because I'm the one that's working through you."

God has a special calling in this regard pertaining to women. Throughout history and across cultures, the world has tried to stereotype women as silly, foolish, inferior, and weak. But in this hour, God has a special plan for women on the front lines of their workplaces, in their homes, and certainly within the church. Your workplace is your personally assigned mission field; your home has been given as a divine haven of rest; and your church is the tabernacle where you come to find strength among other believers, as well as to strengthen those believers, in the unity of the Spirit.

I believe in the last days we are going to see God call more women to the front lines. God will begin to prick women's hearts, begin to put a boldness within them, begin to put a hunger in them, but every good thing that the Lord ordains, Satan comes to destroy. The enemy has his tactics

One Minute of Praise

for derailing those called of God. Especially in the area of boldness, we must not become proud or overbearing. We must ask how we are to use this boldness. We must be very careful that within the church, we as women, no matter where God elevates us to, still remain submitted to our husbands. We must submit to our employers, our pastor, and those in leadership within the church. We must submit to our pastoral staff as we work under them.

No matter what God does in you or through you, you are still a woman under the submission of the leadership that is over you. I understand this because of the calling God placed upon my life. Never in a million years would I have ever dreamed that I would be saying, "Women, God is calling you to the front line." But I also know within my spirit that it is important we keep a sweet attitude—that we stay humble and use what God is pouring through us for His glory. We must be careful not to harm our sister, or our brother, or bring confusion, because I know the devil is out to destroy what God is doing through us. If he can cause us to turn on our sister or our brother and bring them down, tearing apart the body of Christ, then he will be satisfied with what he has managed to do with God's call on our life.

God is calling women to be a temple of His presence. We must continually seek after His Presence because lightness and darkness cannot dwell in the same temple. As long as we house His presence, everything that comes out of our mouths, everything that goes in our ears, every thought

The Glory Within

that goes into our minds will glorify Him. Darkness will not be able to creep in. We cannot play the middle. There are no gray sides with the heavenly Father. Either the presence dwells within you, or darkness dwells within you.

God is calling you, just as he did Mary, to sit at His feet. She understood that outside of His Presence, she was nothing. Her passion for His Presence made her a worshipper after His own heart—just like David—and David's tabernacle that was continually filled with God's Glory.

Lord, help me to seek you with my whole heart. I know that it is only in Your Presence that I will find fullness of joy. I know You have called me to Your Glory, and that Christ alive in me is my only hope of being filled with that Glory everyday. Holy Spirit, lead me back to that place within my heart where I can bask in God's Presence no matter what my circumstances.

One Minute of Praise:

How can you continually be filled with the glory of God? Begin practicing now—for one whole minute:

One Minute of Praise

TWENTY-TWO

A House Undivided Will Not Fall

Behold, how good and how pleasant it is for brethren to dwell together in unity!

Psalm 133:1 NKJV

Everything that God does Satan will try to destroy. On July the fourth of last year—it was a Sunday night—we went home and went to bed, and in the middle of the night I had a dream. In that dream we were in the sanctuary of our church. My husband stepped to the pulpit, and began to direct the service. Suddenly, I looked around and people were in clusters all around the church. Everywhere

I looked they were in groups. Now some were singing, some were talking, some were praying, some were speaking in tongues. What people were doing was not bad; it was just that they were not unified. They were doing their own thing within their groups and no matter what the pastor tried to do, he could not bring them back into unity because everybody was wanting to do their own thing. Suddenly, I saw a lady step out in the aisle. She was a petite lady and as she stepped out, she suddenly fell backwards—and as soon as she fell backwards, she stood straight up stiff as a board. I looked at her and thought, *"There's something wrong with this. I don't understand what this is."* And suddenly this woman looked up and she pointed at my husband and she said, "I am a witch and I have been sent to this church and I will destroy the church. I will destroy the families. And I will destroy their workplaces."

Quickly, with one bounce, my husband leaped to where she was standing. He went right up to her, pointed his finger, and said, "There are no weapons formed against me that can prosper. The Lord says that I've been covered by the blood. When I've been covered by the blood, Satan has nothing on me. God has commanded His angels to have charge over me. And the Lord has promised me that upon this rock I will build my church and the gates of hell will not prevail against it." Suddenly, she blew up in a blast of confetti that came raining down everywhere.

In my dream I was asking the Lord, saying, "I don't understand. A witch? What is a witch? I don't understand." So I went to the Bible and I began to read about witches. I came across this scripture dealing with how rebellion and division is the root of witchcraft. Then the Lord came to me and this is what He said, "Tell my people to guard their minds, their ears, and their tongues. If they will, I will continue to fill their temple with My glory."

See, Satan wants you. He wants your house to be a hellhole. He wants your work to be so stressful that when you come home, you can't even get along with your family. You can't even spend time with your children because you're so exhausted by the end of the day. You can't communicate with your husband because you're too tired. Or your husband just wants to be left alone when he comes home, because the stress of his day has been so heavy.

That's what the enemy wants. He wants the home to be so filled with confusion, and division, and everybody doing their thing—that's how Satan worms his way into the family. That's how he slithers into the workplace. That's how he creeps into the church.

But I have news for you. The Lord says the blood covers everything. There is not a weapon formed against you that Satan used to penetrate your shield. In Psalm 91 we read that he will put a shield of protection around you. I think of it like those clocks where there is a glass dome over the top. Everywhere I go I'm in this dome. When Satan gets his gun out, or gets his water balloons out, or gets his grenades, or whatever he has, it comes and hits that glass and it goes bing, bing, bing and doesn't hurt a thing, because the Word says there is not a weapon that can be formed against me that can prosper.

Thank you Lord that You have equipped and empowered me through Your Holy Spirit to walk in peace. With Your love in my heart, Your words in my mouth, and Your peace that guards my mind in Christ, I can triumph over the striving and confusion that threatens to destroy me.

One Minute of Praise:

Let go of those areas where the enemy has stirred up strife and praise God for His peace prevailing there:

VI.

Praise that Propels You into Your Destiny

TWENTY-THREE

Don't Let Go of Your Promise

Then Jesus told them, "I assure you, if you have faith and don't doubt, you can do things like this and much more. You can even say to this mountain, 'May God lift you up and throw you into the sea,' and it will happen.

Matthew 21:21

*A*re you still praying and believing for a promise that God has birthed in your spirit, but you have yet to see it come to pass? The enemy would love for you to put that promise up on a shelf and forget about it—to stop praying

One Minute of Praise

about it—let the cobwebs and dust smother it, the mice chew on it, and the next thing you know—poof!—it's gone. And you wonder, *I don't understand what happened. Where did my promise go? God, You gave it to me*—but you didn't keep it in your heart.

A promise is not something that instantly fades away. You know when God births something in you and after you've prayed about it, you feel like you could kill every giant that comes in your pathway. That's what happens when you come to the altar. God gives you that supernatural power and you feel like you could get up and go out and there's not a giant you couldn't conquer. But Satan knows how to get you off track. He attacks you in the little things. One by one those little things begin having power over you and before long, that promise that was within your spirit is gone—it has totally faded away.

It's easy for us to put our promises on the shelf when things don't change instantly. We live in a microwave age and are used to having our desires satisfied instantly. We drive up to a burger place and don't even have to get out of the car. We order it, pay for it, and there's our meal. If we have to wait for the car in front of us who doesn't move on instantaneously, we get impatient.

We go to buy popcorn to cook in the microwave and we examine our options saying, "Well, this one takes five minutes. The other only takes three and a half." I'll take the three and a half minute box. We've got to have it now. That's what the world has developed into—and it's no different within the church. We come to church and expect to have a Burger King service saying, "I want it my way, and I want it now."

Let's say you are a person that has an unsaved husband and you have prayed for that devil of a man—sometimes he can be a booger-bear—he's just as mean as can be. You've prayed and you've prayed and God spoke to your spirit and said, "He's going to get saved one day." And you're telling God that He's got a lot more faith than you've got. You're saying, "You don't have to live with him every day like I do." And you continue to pray and pray. But see, with your physical, natural eyes, nothing is changing. However, there's something natural eyes cannot see—in the heavens, there's been warfare going on. You have no idea as you are praying, and as you are believing, and as you are standing on those promises, that there's warfare going on in the heavens for his soul. The key is to stay on your knees, stay in the Word, and believe in your heart that things are going to change. Don't give up. Just because it doesn't happen after three minutes in the microwave, don't give up. Go back and pop it a little longer.

The Holy Spirit comes to you and gives you hope so you can have faith. You've got to have faith. Without faith there's no sense in hoping for anything. If you lose your faith, you might as well lay it all down. You might as well put every promise you've got on the shelf. You might as well pack your bags and go home to live with your parents because without faith nothing is possible—but with faith all things are possible.

Let's look at Matthew chapter 21. Jesus is talking to His disciples here. "Then Jesus told them, 'I assure you, if you have faith and don't doubt...' Say, "Doubt." Circle it. Underline it. Highlight it. That's a tool of the enemy—*doubt.*

"If you have faith and don't doubt, you can do things like this and much more" (Matthew 21:21). The Lord is saying right here that you can do what He's done and much more—but you've got to have faith. It says, "You can say to this mountain, 'May God lift you up and throw you into the sea.'" Now I don't think He meant you could walk up to Mount Rainier and say "Be removed." I believe He meant the mountains in your life. There is not a mountain that Satan can put in front of you that you could not say to it, "I command you be removed in the name of Jesus because in the Gospel of Matthew it is written that if I speak to you, mountain, you will be removed." The mountain has to move. Why? Because it's just been spoken to by the Word of God. Everything has to obey the Word of God.

It says, "May God lift you up and throw you into the sea." Does it say it might happen? Or there's a possibility? Or if we hope it will happen? What does it say? "It shall—*it*

will—happen." No question. There's no doubt about it. It will happen.

But there's a condition. Every mountain will be removed. Everything in your life that's coming against you will only be removed *if* you have faith and speak the Word—*if* you believe that you will receive whatever you ask for in prayer. There's also another condition. You have to pray about it. The Lord says you've got to speak the Word, you've got to have faith, and you've got to pray about it. Then there is nothing—*nothing*—that you can't conquer.

Hallelujah! Thank You, Lord, for Your Word! Thank You Father God for the authority You have given me in Christ Jesus, that greater things than He did shall I do, and that no weapon formed against me will prosper—no mountain will stand between me and victory.

One Minute of Praise:

How awe-inspiring are the promises of God! Think out loud about all that He has promised—for one minute:

TWENTY-FOUR

Setting Sail

And when it was decided that we should sail for Italy, they delivered Paul and some other prisoners to a centurion of the Augustan Cohort named Julius. And embarking in a ship of Adramyttium, which was about to sail to the ports along the coast of Asia, we put to sea.

Acts 27:1,2 ESV

This is the best story I know in the Word that talks about keeping promises before you. In this story, Paul had every reason to wonder where his promise went. He and several other prisoners had been taken into custody. They were with an officer of the army and had been placed on a boat heading toward Rome. This was not just a little paddleboat—

Setting Sail

103

we know there were more than two hundred people on board.

When they started out on this voyage everything seemed to be going fine. The water looked beautiful—very peaceful—there was a cool breeze—and the sun was shining. They were just out for a nice day—as nice as you could have as a prisoner. They were out for a nice cruise in the Mediterranean. They were sailing close to the shore because they had some stops to make along the way. They had these prisoners on board, so they wanted to keep everything in order. They looked down in the water and saw where there was sand, where there were stumps, and where the rocks were. They were able to see everything that could bring harm. They thought, *"Well, we've got it made."* They looked around and began to build up a little confidence. They thought, *"You know, we haven't hit one rock. We haven't gotten caught in any whirlpools."* So their self-confidence began to build.

Then look at Acts 27:13-15

When a light wind began blowing from the south, the sailors thought they could make it. So they pulled up anchor and sailed along close to shore. But the weather changed abruptly, and a wind of typhoon strength (a "northeaster," they called it) caught the ship and blew it out to sea. They couldn't turn the ship into the wind, so they gave up and let it run before the gale.

One Minute of Praise

This didn't just happen. God commanded the wind to arise. Why? Because it was going to bring glory to Him. Why do circumstances come in your life that seem so overwhelming? Because the way you handle it will either bring glory to self (the flesh), or it will bring glory to God.

In verse 19 we read, "The next day, as gale-force winds continued to batter the ship, the crew began throwing the cargo overboard. (Acts 27:18). Little by little, they began to throw their dreams and goals and valuables overboard because their circumstances seemed so much bigger than their promises. If we were in the same situation we might wonder, *"Did we really hear from God? Did He really tell me to start this business? Did He really tell me that this is what I should be doing, or was it my imagination? Was it something that I wanted, or the Lord?"* You need to do a heart search, because if God said it, that settles it—and you just have to believe it and see it through.

Lord God, thank You for causing me to recognize Your voice—and for giving me the fortitude to continually trust in Your promises. I rejoice today knowing Your Glory goes before me and follows after me—I will be blessed going out and coming back again. I thank You for completing the good work You have begun in me and fulfilling every promise and desire You have put in my heart.

One Minute of Praise:

Knowing that God has ordered all things for your benefit, even what seems difficult in the present moment, what can you think to say to Him now?

_____

_____

_____

_____

_____

_____

_____

_____

_____

TWENTY-FIVE

Don't Lose Your Compass

And on the third day they threw the ship's tackle overboard with their own hands. When neither sun nor stars appeared for many days, and no small tempest lay on us, all hope of our being saved was at last abandoned.

Acts 27:19,20 ESV

*I*f you're out at sea and you can't see anything—it's getting dark and the wind is blowing—your compass is the only thing that can get you back to where you came from. The last thing you want to do is throw your compass overboard. When you can't see the sun or stars through the storm clouds, you won't know what direction north, south, east, and west is. That's exactly what happened here; they threw their compass away, which was the one thing they needed to get them back to shore.

What happens to us when Satan strikes and we panic and begin to throw our promises overboard? The first thing we do is to stop reading the Bible. We put it on the shelf because we get too busy trying to solve problems and take care of the situation. We just got too busy. Then, we miss a day in prayer. We miss our morning time in prayer. We miss our evening time in prayer. Now we've gone two days without reading the Word. Now we've gone three days without praying. We find we just need to get away for the weekend—go up to the lake—sit in God's nature and let Him minister to us. And then we wonder, "*Why isn't God taking care of my situation? I know God can turn it around.*" Well, you just threw your compass overboard.

Why is it when we need God the most in our life to change things, that's when we pull away from Him? Does that make any sense? That's how Satan blinds us to get us to feel sorry for ourselves—to get us out of the Word—to get us off our knees. Because when we get out of the Word and get off of our knees, we begin to feel sorry for ourselves. We start to justify every selfish feeling. The enemy will come in and plant doubt and unbelief, which ultimately will turn into discouragement and self-pity. Don't let the devil sell you his discouragement, because if nothing else works in his box of tricks, his discouragement will.

Notice how the storm went on and on? It didn't just blow in and out again. When Satan comes in and he doesn't just come in with a sudden gust. It's a gradual thing. Also, notice that after many days the storm blotted out the sun and stars. The stars and sun didn't just disappear suddenly. It was a gradual thing. The devil has a strategy in taking your promises. He cannot take all of your promises away at once—he takes them one at a time until all of a sudden when you look out, you don't see the sun. You don't see the stars. All you see is the storm in front of you. You're thinking, "Lord, I can't even see-beyond where I am." That's how you backslide because there seems to be nothing else around. There's no hope. That's what causes good people to commit suicide. People that have served the Lord commit suicide because Satan has come in and stolen everything until they have nothing to live for.

Satan loves to magnify the negative no matter what the situation is. He will come and put those binoculars to your face and you'll look through them and all you can see is your problem as it eclipses the Son.

Now look at what happened next: "No one had eaten for a long time. Finally, Paul called the crew together and said, 'Men, you should have listened to me in the first place and not left Fair Havens. You would have avoided all this injury and loss.'" (Acts 27:21.)

Have you ever had the Lord come to you and say, "If you'd have listened to me in the first place, you wouldn't have gotten yourself into this mess"? The best thing to do is to say, "I'm sorry"—but that's hard to say, isn't it?

Now there's nothing left on the ship except people—and there is nothing within the power of the people that can save the ship. There are going to be times in your life that you finally realize there is nothing within your power that can change your situation. You're going to have to rely on the Lord. Of course, if you had learned that earlier in the game, it wouldn't have taken so long to get to that big revelation.

Tape this to your forehead: "When it is fruitless to struggle, it is wisdom to yield." In other words, get back on your knees and get back in the Word. Get back to where you were before. If you will get back in the Word and get back on your knees, God will take care of everything. You might as well hit the carpet because there's nothing left that you can do.

Forgive me, Lord, for those times I've thrown my compass overboard. You are my True North, my North Star, and it is only to You that I look for direction. Help me to stay the course and finish the race without getting sidetracked or stranded. You are my hope and my strong fortress each and every day.

One Minute of Praise:

How does the Lord lead you day by day? What do you know of God regarding his navigational skills? What kind of captain is He? Tell God what your heart is telling you as you answer these questions— for one minute:

_____

_____

_____

_____

_____

_____

_____

_____

_____

TWENTY-SIX

Take Courage!

Yet now I urge you to take heart, for there will be no loss of life among you, but only of the ship. For this very night there stood before me an angel of the God to whom I belong and whom I worship, and he said, Do not be afraid, Paul; you must stand before Caesar. And behold, God has granted you all those who sail with you. So take heart, men, for I have faith in God that it will be exactly as I have been told.

Acts 27:22-25 ESV

$\mathcal{P}$aul is imploring those on this ship to "take courage." Courage requires faith—if you can stir up a little courage, you'll get your faith working and have some hope

One Minute of Praise

of making it. If you have hope, you have a better chance, right? See, hope and faith work together. Now there were two hundred and seventy-six people on board beside themselves with fear and panic, but Paul knew that he wasn't going to die. How did Paul know that he wasn't going to die? Just look at the circumstances: the sun was gone, the stars were gone, the water was coming in the boat. How can Paul stand up and tell this crew to take courage?

Paul preaches a stirring sermon there in the midst of the storm, in the dark and wet, and tells his shipmates to "Take courage." He says to them, "Not one life on board this ship will be lost. Every one of you will make it to shore alive." Now some of those men couldn't swim, I'm sure they were thinking, "He doesn't know I can't swim. The boat is going down and I'm going to survive?" But you see, when God's in it, he makes all things possible. It doesn't make any difference whether you can swim or not. If God's in it, you know there'll be a life raft prepared for you that will come bobbing up alongside of you just when you need it.

Here's what happened to Paul. He said, "Last night an angel of God to whom I belong and whom I serve stood beside me." (Acts 27:23). Now he wasn't way out there where Paul couldn't get to him. He wasn't behind him where Paul couldn't see him. He was right there beside him. Perhaps he even had his arm around him when he said, "Paul, it's going to be okay. You're going to make it. You're going to survive." The angel gave Paul a promise. No matter what the circumstances look like, there is not a storm that can hinder the communication of God's favor to His people. No matter how big the storm, no matter how loud the thunder, no matter how bright and blinding the lightening is overhead; God is always present.

The angel told Paul, "Don't be afraid, for you will surely stand trial before Caesar." Perhaps to the other men that meant absolutely nothing. There are going to be times when the Lord gives you a word and if you share it with someone else they will have no idea what it means. But to you it means the difference between life and death because God has spoken it to your spirit. And here Paul is saying, "Hey guys, I'm going to appear before Caesar!" And the other prisoners are thinking, "Caesar is going to kill you. You might as well die now because if you don't, you're going to die when you get to Rome." But Paul is thinking, "You don't know what my God has promised me. You don't know what the Lord has spoken to me about where He's going to take me from here." You see, nothing could stand in Paul's way of the promise that God had given to him.

Help me, Lord, not to lose heart. Thank You for Your Word that encourages me, for Your ministers and teachers that urge me to "take courage" when I can't see Your promises for myself through the storms blowing around me. Thank You for Your angels and Your Holy Spirit that are ever present with me, bringing me the good news of Your faithfulness.

One Minute of Praise

One Minute of Praise:

What is it that gives you courage? How can you "take heart" during life's stormiest times?

_____

_____

_____

_____

_____

_____

_____

_____

_____

TWENTY-SEVEN

Keeping A Praise Perspective

But striking a reef, they ran the vessel aground. The bow stuck and remained immovable, and the stern was being broken up by the surf.

Acts 27:41 ESV

The boat runs aground and begins to break apart. Everybody's out there bobbing in the water. It's dark. Isn't it amazing that they found land? But you know, it's amazing how God comes in and turns circumstances around. We may not understand it but God has a way of doing it. We do not read in here that it says, "Well, there was one that perished—the one who couldn't swim." Every life was saved. There is not a problem, there is not a circumstance, and there is not a situation in your life that is too big for God. He can change anything.

The story continues from the ship breaking apart. They finally get on land and they're shouting, "Boys, we've made it. We finally got here. We will live now." Paul comes up out of that water dripping wet, tired, and hungry—completely worn out. And what happens when he walks up on the shoreline? A snake bites him. I'm sure Paul thought, "Can you believe this? I survive a shipwreck, and I die from a snakebite."

Sometimes God takes you through a trial. It's like old booger-bear; your husband, finally gets saved, then all of a sudden, he loses his job. You're thinking, "God, I can't believe You finally bring my husband into church; he finally gives his life to You and now he loses his job. Lord, he's going to wonder, 'Well God, what did You do that for?'" It's another testing time. The enemy comes to steal your victory, rain on your parade, pluck up any revelation or faith-affirming experience, but don't lose heart because it's really only Satan's last ditch effort to distract you from the truth of your salvation.

Paul was not going to let that serpent come up and bite him, and cause him to give up and say, "Well boys, it's nice being with you all. As I take my last breath, y'all remember me when you go to Caesar." No. He still had the promise:

"You will appear before Caesar." If God has given you a promise about blessing your finances, blessing your home, bringing your children back into church, bringing everybody in your home into the fold, don't give up no matter what Satan throws at you. It's your choice. Because you know what Paul did? I believe he said, "Lord, if You brought me this far, You're not going to let me down now."

All that happened to Paul did not bring glory to him, it brought glory to the One that he served. When the snakebite didn't hurt him, revival hit that island. Now he had a choice. He could have let the circumstance take him under and give it up and allow those people to die and go to hell. But he said, "Lord, no matter what, I'm going to serve You. No matter if I'm out by the gate like Job. No matter if I'm in a shipwreck. I'm going to keep the promise before me that You said I will make it. Your household can be saved. And there's nothing, no circumstance, nothing that is going to prevail against you. You must stand on His Word. I'm going to believe it come shipwreck or snakebite." You can make it through a shipwreck and survive a snake bite. His Word is your life raft and your antidote.

Even though Paul was a prisoner, Paul became a counselor and a comforter in a time of struggle. When a struggle comes to you, what do you do? When people are around you, what vibes do they get from you? Do you exude gloom and despair so that people feel sorry for you? Or do others say, "Boy, I tell you what. They are so rooted.

I can't understand how they can go through this battle. I can't understand how their child's life could be taken away and they come to church with their hands raised and they say, 'Lord, I give You glory. I praise You. I magnify You. I don't understand the things on this earth, but I know one day I will stand before You. One day You and I will meet face to face.'" But they will only say this if everything going on in your life is bringing glory to the Lord—if in the midst of turmoil; you chose to become a comforter.

In verse 24 we read, "What's more, God in his goodness has granted safety to everyone sailing with you." We can either bring people up with us, or drag them down to defeat with us. How you react to circumstances affects other people. Everybody has an influence on somebody. You will either bring people up or bring them down. One day you will stand before God and be judged for whether you brought people to the Lord as a comforter and counselor, or you pulled them away from the cross to focus on you or your problems.

The Lord is saying, "It's not what it appears to be." You're circumstance cannot dictate the outcome. Paul's circumstance seemed so hopeless, but you know that storm wasn't what it appeared to be. It appeared to be disaster. It appeared that everybody was going to die. But did Paul ever focus on what he was seeing with his natural eyes, "Boy, the waves are getting awful high. It sure is getting dark out here." No. He walked around saying, "Boys, take courage! Come on! Take courage. We're going to make it."

 Keeping A Praise Perspective 119

In your circumstance are you focusing on the waves coming in and splashing around you? How do you react to those circumstances? I promise you with a money back guarantee, when situations come in your life and the devil throws water in your face; it is not what it appears to be. He's a liar. He's a deceiver and it's through lies and deception that he kills, steals, and destroys. Your circumstance, no matter how bad it seems, is not what it appears to be.

Hallelujah! Praise You Lord for Your hand on my life! Thank You that all is working out for my good because I love You and praise You! I lift up Your Name and rejoice in You, my God, my only hope and my salvation. You alone are worthy of my attention, and my praise. You alone can turn the tide of my situation.

One Minute of Praise:

Think for a minute, one whole minute, about the hope you have in Christ.

TWENTY-EIGHT

An Angel Story

That evening the two angels came to the entrance of the city . . .

Genesis 19:1

*O*ne of my favorite illustrations has to do with an older angel and a younger angel who were sent to earth on assignment. When they were sent down to the earth the Lord said to them, "You're assignment is to go into a very wealthy neighborhood—to a particular house of a very wealthy man who has multiple garages, multiple cars, multiple bedrooms, multiple bathrooms—a large, large estate—and you're to spend the night with him tonight."

The angels made their way through the neighborhood and at last the Lord said, "This is the house." They looked up to see an enormous house—the kind that has the big glass windows in front so you can see the chandelier hanging down over the staircase. They walked up and rang the doorbell. The man came to the door wearing his silk pajamas and his fur slippers. When he answered the door they said, "Sir, would you by chance have a place for us to sleep tonight? We're very tired, and weary. Would you by chance have a bed where we could sleep?"

The gentleman stood there for a few minutes and then he said, "Oh, sure, come on in." So he took them downstairs to a very dark, dingy, damp basement where there was an old cot. It's late, so they get ready for bed. During the night the younger angel hears the older angel up. When he looks around, the older angel has walked over to the side of the room and is looking at a big hole in the wall. He looks at the hole and with his hands he begins to close in the hole.

When morning comes, it's time to move on to their next mission. The Lord says to them, "Tonight you're going to go out in the country on a dirt road to a little white frame house. You're going to go to an elderly couple that does not have much and spend the night with them."

So they make their way out to the country. Their feet become very hot and tired from walking. Finally, they walk up to the little picket fence, and up the little stone sidewalk. When they get up to the house they see the screen door is kind of half on and half off. They rattle the door until an older gentleman and woman come to answer. The older angel again inquired,

"Would you by chance have a place for my friend and me to spend the night tonight? We're very, very tired" Without any hesitation they say, "Oh, yes. We have a bed. You can have our bed. My wife and I will sleep on the couch. Please stay, we'd be honored to have you spend the night with us tonight."

So they go inside and go to bed. When the angels wake up the next morning, they hear weeping and crying. They listen and the younger angel hears the woman in the kitchen sitting at the table weeping and saying, "I don't know what we're going to do. Our dairy cow was all that we had and she died last night. How are we going to survive? What are we going to do?"

And the younger angel looked at the older angel and said, "I don't understand? How could you allow this to happen? The night before last we stayed in that big house with all those fine bedrooms throughout the house and we are put in the basement to sleep on a cot. You walk over and perform a miracle by closing a hole in his wall. Now we're in a poor farmhouse and you let the cow die! You've got the power. You could have stopped it."

The older angel looked at the younger angel and said, "You don't understand. It's not what it appears to be. You see, in the big house the millionaire had taken all of his money and his gold and his silver and he had hidden it in the wall. With one hand I closed it in so that never again will he have it. Last night the death angel came for the farmer's wife and I talked the death angel into taking the cow instead."

An Angel Story

When circumstances come into your life and seem so overwhelming, and you say, "I don't understand." Remember, it's not what it appears to be. When the devil comes and slaps you in the face when it seems you were doing so well, don't lose hope. Perhaps you suddenly lose your job, not knowing God has a better job for you. You cannot understand all that transpires in the course of a day. You cannot know what tomorrow holds. You can only try to understand what has happened in the past. You cannot change the past, but you can affect your future by staying the course and trusting God. The choice is yours.

Holy Spirit, help me keep an eternal perspective. In this moment, as I meditate on Your goodness, I can see that You are ordering my steps. Remind me, Lord, when confusion and chaos strike, to be still and know that You are God.

One Minute of Praise:

How many times have circumstances not turned out as they appeared they would? Might God have had something to do with it? Take a minute to remind yourself of His faithfulness—and praise Him for it.

TWENTY-NINE

Divine Preparation

No eye has seen, no ear has heard, and no mind has imagined what God has prepared for those who love him.

1 Corinthians 2:9

The summer of my fourteenth year, I went to church camp. I was amazed to see kids praying and weeping at the altar and being filled with the Holy Spirit. One of those nights, I became so hungry for God—I wanted to experience what all of the others were experiencing—so I stayed at the altar and sought the Lord. What I didn't know was that the Lord was preparing me for a life-altering situation I was soon to face. I stayed there at the altar until four o'clock in the morning.

 Divine Preparation

During that week the Lord gave me three promises. He said, "One day I'm going to use your musical ability to bring glory to Me." Now you've got to understand, I had never had music lessons. At that time, I could only play in the key of C. On occasion, I might break out into the key of F, but that was it. I learned to play *There is a Fountain* and *Amazing Grace*. We sang those two songs every Sunday in our little Foursquare Church in either the key of C or F.

So when the Lord told me one day my musical ability would be used for Him, I didn't quite understand it. But by faith I said, "God, if You said it, I believe it."

He said next, "One day you're going to marry a preacher." Now I liked that. I remembered that all through high school, and when I graduated, I decided the best place to find a preacher was at Bible school. I thought, "God, I'm going to help You out on this one." There was a junior college near the Bible school and so I enrolled there. The rest is history. God sent me a wonderful preacher man.

The last thing He said to me was, "You're going to travel to many places. You're going to travel all over the world and share Jesus." Well, at that time we didn't even own a car. We didn't think we would ever have enough money to own a car. My parents walked to work and I walked to school. Yet God was saying, "One day you're going to play the piano and the organ, and you're going to travel all over the world." Honestly, I didn't even know how I was going to get out of the town I lived in. But as a teenager, God spoke these things into my tender little spirit. I wrote them down and everyday I would pray, "God, this is what You promised me," though the circumstances I was living in did not give me much hope of ever achieving much for God.

Several months after returning from that camp my life drastically changed. When I was at home, in the month of October, I suddenly heard this very loud sound coming from the bedroom—like someone gasping for breath. I swung open the door and found my dad lying on the bed. His face had turned totally black. He was having a massive heart attack and was dying. My dad and I were very, very close. I began to scream out to God. I begged Him to spare his life. If there were any words to be prayed, I prayed them until there weren't any more left to pray. I could not understand. I ask the Lord, "God, why are you taking the most precious thing from me?" But in a still, small voice He said to me, "You don't understand. It's not what it appears to be."

See, in these small towns, everybody knows everybody. When my father suddenly passed away from a massive heart attack, there were so many flowers sent to our home that there wasn't room to put them all. We had to request no more be sent. There was a Baptist Church there that said, "You know, this family has very little money. The chances are slim that this girl will ever have a chance to go to college, so let's open a trust fund, and put the money from the people who still want to send flowers into that trust fund—

 Divine Preparation

and then one day, perhaps, she will have a chance to go to college."

By the time I graduated from high school, there was enough money in that fund to pay for my first year of college. So my mother and I went together to Waxahachie, Texas, with twenty dollars in our pocket, no job, and nowhere to live. We decided to go there because we had some friends that were going to school there and we were able to stay overnight at their house.

The next day, one of the girls came to my mom and said, "Mary, you might want to go to the cafeteria because I just got word today that they're looking for a supervisor." My mother went right over, and the next day she started working in the cafeteria at the college. She worked there for the next twenty-one years.

When she got off work at the college, she looked across the street and saw a house for rent. She came to me and said, "Let's go check on this house." The next day we move into that house and I lived there with her until I got married.

You see the price that I had to pay to get where I am today? Yes, it was a high price because I lost the most precious thing in the world to me—my father. Remember the Lord saying to me, you don't understand. It's not what it appears to be. If your father lived, you you would live in this city for the rest of your life." But God said, "I have something bigger and better planned for you. I knew you by name when you were in your mother's womb. I designed your day. I anointed you."

I'm no different than you. God says, "I have a purpose for each one of you. I've called you by name. I've chosen you. I've set you apart. But you've allowed things to come into your life. You've allowed situations to steal your promises—to destroy them. You have allowed your promises to be put up on the shelf." But God is saying, "It's time to resurrect those promises." If God's given them to you, they will come to pass. It's a choice. OK, you put them on a shelf or do you hang onto them and say, "Satan, it's not what it appears to be. I know if God's Word said it, I know I can claim it, and I know that it's going to happen just the way He promised." The choice is yours. Are you going to allow the enemy to conquer you, beat you up, knock you down, and destroy you, or are you going to stand up and say, "Lord, I choose to have courage in You. You give me hope. You said I will survive. There's not a demon in hell, there's not a man on this earth, that can steal Your promise because what You have given me, nobody, nobody, nobody can steal from me. What your Lord has blessed, no man can curse."

Where is your promise? Intercessors, when you pray and pray and pray and you don't see anything changing, you just remember it's not what it appears to be. God is still working. God is still bringing His promises to pass.

I know the Lord has spoken into your spirits saying, "I've given you promises that you have forgotten about them." Some of you need to go back and reclaim the promises God has given you. The devil has stolen your joy. He's stolen your

Divine Preparation

victory—just like he's stolen your family, he's stolen your job, he's stolen your home, or he's stolen your finances. Stake claim to get them back and say to the devil, "Enough is enough!"

If you'll be sensitive to His Spirit, you'll discern that many times God is preparing you for something greater. He is preparing you so that when the blocks get knocked out from underneath you, it's not much of a jolt. God is always preparing you for victory.

You are the God of all wisdom. I trust that You are carefully ordering my steps and preparing me for all that You would have me do for You. Thank You, Lord, for Your watchful eye and grace to overcome. I will hold tight to the promises You have given me and continue to trust in Your faithfulness as I patiently wait to see every one fulfilled.

One Minute of Praise:

Remember all of the times God has proven Himself faithful. Remind yourself of His steadfast love and unwavering faithfulness—for one minute:

VII.

Mountain Moving
Praise

THIRTY

Praise Believes

And Jesus answered them, Have faith in God. Truly, I say to you, whoever says to this mountain, Be taken up and thrown into the sea, and does not doubt in his heart, but believes that what he says will come to pass, it will be done for him. Therefore I tell you, whatever you ask in prayer, believe that you have received it, and it will be yours.

Mark 11:22-24 ESV

"*H*ave faith in God. For verily I say unto you, That whosoever shall say unto this mountain...." What does He say we should say? "Be thou removed, and be thou cast into the sea." There are certainly some of you who need to look at your mountains and tell them where to go! Do you understand what I mean? Some of you are facing some real issues. But at the same time, some of you are facing mountains that only look like mountains, but they are really just "weapons of distraction" sent by the enemy.

Have you ever been to Warner Brothers or MGM out in California? You walk onto these stage sets that look like beautiful neighborhoods. There are beautiful homes on the right, and beautiful homes on the left. They have the driveways and sidewalks, and you almost want to live there. But if you step over just a few feet, you'll see the houses are really just a bunch of two by fours holding up giant facades. They're just propping up a big picture of a beautiful house.

That's what many of the mountains you face in your life really are. Satan is back there propping up a bunch of painted cardboard cutouts—stuff he's put together to make you think you're looking at Mount Everest. You think you'll never get over it, around it, or under it—when it's just a big piece of painted cardboard. But if he can get you to think it's a mountain in your mind, to make you think your faith is too small to handle it, he knows he has you. Instead, it's time to take authority over that mountain and see it as the weapon of distraction that it is—then speak to it and tell it to be removed.

Have faith in God. Speak to that mountain and tell it to be removed and be cast into the sea. Do not doubt in your heart. Say out loud, "I will not doubt in my heart." Do not doubt in your heart but believe. Say, "Believe." Believe that those things you are praying for *shall* come to pass. (See Mark 11:22-23.)

You will have whatever you speak as long as you believe and have the faith to receive it. Many of us are still walking around with sick bodies—I didn't say everyone because there are different cases for different situations—But many of us are walking around with sick bodies, and with homes in disarray, with financial troubles, simply because we have not spoken in faith. What do you speak? You speak what God's Word says, and we have to believe it! We have got to speak that Word out. We need to stop talking about the problem and start talking about the provision.

Jesus said, "Therefore I say unto you, what things soever ye desire, when ye pray, believe that ye receive them, and ye shall have them." Do you realize anything that you pray for you can have as long as you have set up the atmosphere for it? Many times we don't get what we ask for because we haven't set the atmosphere up for it. Too often we think it is like going to the ATM. We get our little spiritual card out and we stick our want card in there and say, "God, this is what I need." Then we pull it out and think God is going to just shoot it out the little slot. But it doesn't work that way. You've got to do some carpet time—you've got to have a few tears streaking down your cheeks and a little snot coming out of your nose. God wants to know your desire is heartfelt and genuine. He wants to know if you will continue to seek Him for it in faith, or compromise and get it another way when He tells you to be patient. Which do you have more faith in? God's Word to you, or something else that promises your answer faster?

Teach me, Lord, to walk in greater faith. Teach me, Holy Spirit, to speak with boldness and authority to the mountains that loom up around me. Help me to see them for what they really are and to conquer each mountain, every distraction the enemy throws up, with Your peace and grace. Help me, Father God, to know when to yield and when to stand firm.

One Minute of Praise:

What are some of the mountains catching your gaze today? Will you sit and ponder them, looking in awe at their size, or will you march around them praising God as the Israelites did around the walls of Jericho? Take the next sixty seconds to do a little marching:

_____

_____

_____

_____

_____

Praise Believes

THIRTY-ONE

A Story of Tenacious Praise

Let us hold fast the confession of our hope without wavering, for He who promised is faithful.

Hebrews 10:23 ESV

*P*astor Darlene Bishop tells a story about a man by the name of Tom Brooks. He was unlearned and illiterate, but had gone to church and had given his heart to the Lord. One day, he heard his pastor say in one of his sermons that all things are possible to those who believe.

"Well," Tom said, "That's pretty simple. All—not part, not just a little bit—but *all* things are possible to them that believe." So he went home to his mother and told her,

One Minute of Praise

"Now mother, I can't read. I've never gone to school to learn how. But my pastor today told me that if I'd ask anything in His name, and if I would believe in my heart, He would give me the desires of my heart because all things are possible to them that believe. So I'm believing that God is going to teach me how to read this Bible."

His mamma said, "Now Tom, you haven't been to school. You haven't got no learning. But they have a class down the street that you could walk to. You could go to school there. They'll teach you how to read. Why don't you just go register in the school because you know, you're really asking for an impossible thing. Let's go down because I know they're teaching people how to read."

Tom said, "But mamma, if I go enroll in that school then what my pastor said ain't true because my pastor said, '*All* things are possible to them that believe.' And *all* things means that if I can't read, and I can ask God, then He will teach me how to read." So he said, "You just stay right here. I'm getting my Bible and I'm going out in the woods back behind our house. I'll be back when I can read."

His mamma thought, "We'll never see Tom again."

So he got his Bible and went out in the woods. He opened it up and stared at the pages. He built a fire and sat by it throughout the night. During the day, he walked in the woods and just stared at those pages. All the while he repeated to himself, "All things are possible to them that believe. All things are possible." He'd turn the page and say again, "All things are possible to them that believe." He'd turn again and pray, "All things are possible to them that believe. God, You said in Your Word that if I ask anything in Your name, it's mine. So all things are possible to them that believe. God, I'm praying that You will teach me to read the Word." So he'd look at it again. He would turn page after page and say, "All things are possible to them that believe."

So one night around the campfire, he had his Bible opened to the Psalms. He looked down at the pages saying, "All things are possible to them that believe. The Lord is my shepherd. I shall not want for He leadeth me beside the still water. He restoreth my soul. He maketh me to lie down in green pastures."

At that, he ran out of the forest shouting to his mother, "Mamma, Mamma listen to this, 'The Lord is my shepherd.'" He ran through the neighborhood waking everybody up by shouting, "Do you hear this? I can read! I can read! 'He maketh me to lie down in green pastures.'"

Don't tell Tom that God can't supply your needs because he knows differently.

But the story doesn't end there. God saved him, filled him with the Spirit, taught him how to read, and then called him to preach. So Tom needed a church to pastor. Again he went to his mother and said, "Mamma, I'm saved. I'm filled with the Spirit. I can read the Word. Now Mamma, I want to build a church."

One Minute of Praise

"Well, now son, you know we haven't got any land and haven't got any money."

"Well, Mamma, that mountain out in front of our house. That mountain right there."

She said, "Are you talking about that real tall mountain?"

"Yeah, the one that you can hardly see the top of. I'm going to build a church there."

"Now Tom, you can't put no church up on top of that mountain."

"No, but let me tell you what I've recently read in the Word. The Word told me that I could speak to my mountain and it could be removed. And I could cast it away and it would have to leave. So Mamma, I'm going back to the woods."

So Tom went back to the woods. The first time he had been out there for eight days before he had his breakthrough. This time it didn't take quite as long. He wasn't out in the woods long declaring, "All things are possible to them that believe. I speak to that mountain and I command that mountain to go now. I cast it away." While he was praying the scripture someone came knocking on his mamma's door. When she answers it, the two men standing there asked, "Mrs. Brooks?"

"Yes."

"We're from a company that's been strip-mining out here on the other side the mountain. We're through strip-mining and we have this big hole in the ground. So we need some dirt. We were wondering, could we have the dirt from your mountain? We'll pay you to move your mountain."

Mamma turns and runs out the back door shouting, "Tom, Tom, your mountain has just moved."

So Tom's mountain was removed, and with the money he got for it, he built his church.

Don't tell Tom that God does not supply all of your needs. He knows better.

You see, Tom created an atmosphere of faith. He took himself away from people—even the person he loved the most—to get alone with God and create an atmosphere in which he could speak to that mountain and it would be removed. And he did it through praise and speaking God's Word.

Hallelujah! Praise You Lord that all things are possible for those who believe! Thank You Lord for giving me the authority in Your Name to move mountains! Thank You Father God for supplying all of my needs according to Your riches in glory! Hallelujah! I rejoice in You today and thank You that You have given me all things pertaining to life and godliness.

One Minute of Praise:

What better reason to rejoice than knowing that "all things are possible?" What things can you think of that would fall under that category? Praise the Lord now for all those things!

THIRTY-TWO

A Weapon of Warfare

For the weapons of our warfare are not of the flesh
but have divine power to destroy strongholds.

2 Corinthians 10:4 ESV

The Word of God is not just a collection of poems, songs, and stories that come from God. The other day I asked myself, "What does the Word mean to me?" This is what I wrote down in my journal, "The words in this book are heaven-sent, life-changing, sin-killing, disease-healing, marriage-restoring, drug-addict-delivering, soul-saving, doubt-delivering, Holy Ghost-filling, esteem-building, fire-breathing, devil-killing, root-plucking, and butt-kicking." The Word of God is sharper than a two-edged sword. It pierces into the mind, the soul, and the heart of man, which makes even the lowliest into vessels of honor (see Hebrews 4:12).

We're all familiar with the story of David and Goliath. We all learned that story in Sunday school, but as I read that story now, the one thing I see when I hear Goliath speaking is that for days he had blasphemed God. In the Old Testament, anyone that blasphemed God was stoned to death. Remember the story of Ahab? How Ahab wanted Naboth's vineyard? So Jezebel got two men to lie saying Naboth had blasphemed God and what happened to him? They stoned him to death. In the Old Testament, no one lived who blasphemed God.

The book of 1 Samuel tells us that Goliath had blasphemed God for days and days and days and no one stood up to him. Then along comes little David saying, "God, he's blasphemed You every day! Anyone that blasphemes You must be stoned to death." So he goes to the creek. I think when he was picking up stones, he wasn't just picking up stones—he was also picking up the Word of God. When he picked up the first stone he said, "All things are possible to them that believe." With the second he said, "My God shall supply all of my needs." Then he picked up another one and said, "I speak to that mountain and I command it to be gone." At the fourth one he said, "You are the Lord God. Is there anything too difficult for You?" And with the fifth one, "Greater is He that is within me than he that is in the world." Then he took that last stone, placed it into his slingshot, and said, "I speak to that mountain." As he began to sling it around and around and around, he said, "Mountain, I command you to come down." Then he walked toward Goliath declaring, "I come to you in the name of the Lord. It's not mine but it's His,"—and he let go of that rock and that rock hit Goliath right in the forehead.

I can see Goliath. I'm not really sure if that stone killed him right then or not, but I see him when it first hit him. He must have staggered. He must have been stunned. He must have been shaken because it says he fell face forward. Usually, if someone hits you in the head, you'll fall backward. I think he was just stunned and knocked loo-loo. So he staggered and fell forward. We know from the story that David then came and took Goliath's very own sword—the sword that he was going to kill the Jews with—and cut Goliath's head off.

Your worship and praise stuns the enemy, but it doesn't annihilate him. It does not destroy him. It does what David's stone did. It stuns and causes him to stagger. But let me tell you what does annihilate the enemy. It's what sharpens that two-edged sword that we read about—that pierces through the darkness and thunder and noise to the heart, the soul, and the mind. It's the Word of God!

Like I said previously, when you read the Word and you hide it inside of you, it sharpens one side of the Sword. But when you start speaking that Word out, you sharpen the other side of the sword. First you put it into your heart and

 A Weapon of Warfare 143

then speak it out of your mouth—in and out, in and out. Suddenly, you have a sword that will bring down any giant in your life.

Many of you are trying to bring down the enemy with one small rock and all you're doing is stunning him. You go to church or attend a conference. You feel like you can conquer anything because the presence of God is so awesome. He comes down and He touches you. He changes you. But the thing is, when you leave and you go back home, the first day, the second day, and the third day you're conquering giants. You're bringing them down. But after a short while, you let the enemy come up against you and suddenly you step back and you're shaken. You're stunned when he hits you with one of his rocks because you've let the Word grow dull inside you. You've stopped putting fresh Word in, so nothing powerful is coming out. Nothing can come out of you that has not been put in you.

Get in the Word. I promise you, if you study in the Word, everything you receive, every anointing that has been imparted into you, will intensify. It will grow greater and greater until no demon in hell will be able to stop you from fulfilling your destiny and accomplishing all God's called you to do.

Father, thank you for equipping me to overcome all of my enemies. Thank you for making me more than a conqueror in Christ. Holy Spirit, I ask you

today to make me mindful of Your Word in my heart and my mouth. Help me not to neglect sharpening the sword of Your Word by meditating on it day and night, and speaking it out in psalms and hymns and spiritual songs. Help me to make the most of every opportunity to bring You glory and praise.

One Minute of Praise:

Let the Word dwell in you richly. Return that living Word to God by speaking it forth. Speak it out in your own, unique psalm right now—for one minute.

A Weapon of Warfare

THIRTY-THREE

Praise Never Backs Down

And without faith it is impossible to please him, for whoever would draw near to God must believe that he exists and that he rewards those who seek him.

Hebrews 11:6 ESV

On December 22, 2003, we received a phone call that my daughter had gone into labor. Our grandson, Chase, was born three months premature. He only weighed two pounds and ten ounces. Of course, you know with a baby that small there's health issues because the lungs and other organs are undeveloped.

So we arrived at the hospital around four o'clock in the morning. As I was in the room with my daughter, the doctor came in and he sat down. When he came in, sat down, crossed his legs, and folded his arms; you know he's about to say something very serious. He told us that they had done everything they could do. "We've got him on a ventilator, plus we are hand-bagging him." They had the oxygen turned up one hundred percent, but his stats were still dropping. So he suggests we put our daughter in a wheelchair and take her to see him for the last time, because they didn't think he would live.

We went into the intensive care room to see him. There was this tiny naked body lying there—just bones with a little bit of flesh on them and almost no muscle tissue whatsoever. He looked so lifeless.

We pushed my daughter up to the side of his bed. The nurse looked at her and said, "Honey, it's okay. You can touch him and you can kiss him goodbye."

The fear was intense. Have you ever been there when suddenly fear grips you? It's like it sinks in and grabs your heart before you can stop it. So I backed up and I looked at the situation. Everything was going through my mind at once, "He's not going to live. He's going to die. There's no way. They've done all they can do." The fear so gripped my heart I began to cry out, "God, please don't let him die. Please don't let him die. Please don't let him die. Please don't let him die. Oh God, please don't let him die. Oh God, God,"—begging and pleading with God.

Have you ever been in a situation where you can't think of anything to say and seem to have nothing to pray. You just begin to scream and beg and try to think of the right words to break through to heaven. Suddenly, Satan said to me, "Remember, standing over your dad's body at fourteen when you walked into the bedroom and he'd had a massive heart attack? You looked down at him and suddenly you began to cry, 'God, please don't let him die. Please don't let him die. Please don't let him die.' Listen to you. You're saying the same words now that you prayed over your daddy's body then and what happened to him? He died. What makes you think this prayer is going to be any different than the prayer you prayed when you were fourteen?"

Suddenly, the fear squeezed even tighter. But thank goodness for the Holy Spirit because in that instant He stepped in and said, "Hold on, just a minute. You didn't have the power and authority at fourteen that you have now. You didn't have the Word in you at fourteen that you have in you now. You didn't have the Holy Ghost in you at fourteen that you have in you now. You didn't have the power to overcome and speak to that mountain at fourteen that you have now. You have been equipped. You have been called. You have been anointed. You have been set apart. Now you take that authority and you use it."

I backed up and I looked at that baby and I said, "By the authority and the power that God has given me, I speak to death and I say, mountain, be thou removed!" It wasn't easy, however, I fought a tremendous battle within my spirit. I was going through a battle because fear and faith were fighting within me for territory. Then the Lord spoke to me and said, "You have no time because time is of essence here. You have no time to get on the phone and call anyone as a backup. You must make your choice this very minute—whether you choose fear or you choose faith—whatever you choose will be the difference between life and death." Thank God I had enough Word in me to choose faith, and Chase lived.

Some of you reading this will have to make a similar choice before this day is over. It's going to make the difference between life and death in a marriage, in a relationship, in your finances, in a job, or regarding your addictions or bad habits. There is a war going on with your spirit between fear and faith, life and death. Every time Satan comes and reminds you of your past, you remind him of all that God has done in you since then.

There are lots of tests in life. When we go through tests, God says, "Now there won't be any cheating while taking your test." But let me tell you what, all God's tests are open book, and although I'm not one who takes tests well, I can pass an open book test anytime. Thank goodness that every test He gives us is an open book test, and that every answer is in *the* Book.

On December twenty-second, we had a mountain. We had a choice. That mountain could overtake us, or we could come against that mountain and use the Word that had been put in us to command it to come down. On that day that mountain was defeated by the Word of God.

How precious is Your Word, O God! How sweet to the soul is Your Word of peace, and how treacherous to the enemy is Your Word of truth. I will rest in You knowing that at Your Word my enemies must flee and my mountains must tumble into the sea. Thank You, Lord, for all the provision I'll ever need—Your eternal, living, life-giving Word.

One Minute of Praise:

What a precious gift we have been freely given. Not only do we have the gift of the Holy Spirit, but we have the Word of God to reveal the many dimensions of all we have inherited in Christ. How blessed we are to have the ability, and the freedom, to soak our souls in the Word of God everyday. Praise God for His Word.

THIRTY-FOUR

Praise with A Vision

Where there is no prophetic vision the people cast off restraint.

Proverbs 29:18 ESV

When God gave Joseph his dream, He showed him his brothers bowing down before him. Isn't it interesting how in the dream, God didn't show him the pit or the prison, He only showed him the promise because He knew if He gave him the promise that no matter what he went through, he would hang onto that promise?

For some of you, all you can focus on is the pit and the prison you are in right now. You have forgotten all about the promise in your heart. You have dropped your dream.

Get your promise off the shelf. Get your promise out of the sack. Get your promise out of the dirty clothes hamper. Get your promise out of the back yard. Go dig it up. It's time to dust off your dream and start pursuing it again.

God only showed Joseph a vision of where he would ultimately end up and not all that he would have to go through to get there. God gave Joseph just enough so he could know the truth in his heart. If you can hang on to the seed of the promise and continue to believe in your heart against all odds, then you will have the faith to overcome your circumstances as well. No great victories were ever won without a great battle. When you hang on to your promise through unrelenting faith, you create an atmosphere in your life for God to work on your behalf.

There are three sharp points that will create the atmosphere you'll need to speak to your mountain:

Keep faith alive in your heart. How do you have faith in your heart? It comes by putting the Word in your heart; because out of the heart, the mouth speaks. Don't beg God with your prayers because begging does not move heaven. Believing the Word that lives in your heart does.

Keep faith alive in your mind. Philippians 4:8 tells us to think on pure things. When something comes into your mind that is not pleasing to your heavenly Father, immediately replace it with a clean thought. It's not wrong to think on it the first time, but it becomes a sin when you don't take those thoughts captive before they enter your mind the second or third time.

Keep faith alive in your eyes. That would be your promise, dream, or vision. Without a vision, your dream will perish. You have heard it said, "What comes out of your mouth you become," because what comes out of your mouth goes into your ears and into your mind and down into your spirit.

Be careful about who you hang around. Some of you are going to need to break off relationships with people because all they do is impart bad things into your thought life and spirit. You've got to break them off if you want to live victoriously. Watch over the atmosphere you create around you. Be diligent about guarding your heart, your mind, and your eyes. Keep your focus on the promise God has given you, and on the God who gave it.

Father God, thank you for Your vision in my heart, mind, and eyes. Help me to see as You see, to love what You love, and to focus only on You and Your promises to me. Thank you for completing the good work You've begun in my life and for being the finisher of my faith. You are everything to me. Without you, I can do nothing, however, with You, all things are possible.

One Minute of Praise:

Think about all the possibilities available to you in Christ. Dare to dream. Praise God for His dream in you, and all you can accomplish in Him—for one minute.

_____

_____

_____

_____

_____

_____

_____

_____

VIII.

Perfected through Praise

THIRTY-FIVE

In Due Season

And let us not grow weary while doing good, for in due season we shall reap if we do not lose heart.

Galatians 6:9 NKJV

God has given you a word, but if you're like me, over time you've become worn down. You've begun losing your patience. You're thinking, "Lord, I can't wait any longer." You've become a little frustrated with God. But be careful, there's great danger in becoming impatient with God. God has designed a destiny for you. He has directed your path towards it. Your steps have been created and designed for you alone, and He alone can direct them. Be careful that you don't take your destiny into your own hands and try to make it happen in your own timing. Let

One Minute of Praise

God order the steps He has prepared before you. Pray for situations without taking them into your own hands and out of God's. Resist becoming impatient and forcing your promise. Honestly, if you do it in your timing and not God's timing, I promise you, things will get really ugly.

Galatians 6:9 says, "And let us not grow weary whiledoing good: for in due season we shall reap if we do not lose heart." Due season may be tomorrow. It may be next month. It may be next year. It may be five years down the road. Due season does not mean taking your bag of popcorn, putting it in the microwave, pressing "popcorn," and it's ready in three minutes. It doesn't mean that you are in desperate need of a job because you're not completely satisfied in your current one—don't walk out expecting God to give you a new job before the week is over.

Something that I've learned about God is that whether it's in my spiritual walk or whether it's just taking care of the natural man, God does not promote anybody until they are overqualified. You might want a promotion within the church or at your workplace, but you are not yet overqualified where you are right now. You've got to work to become overqualified. When you're working, even though you hate your job, you hate your employer, or you hate your co-workers, you must do the best job you can do no matter what. Maybe others are ugly to you. It doesn't matter. Remember, they didn't give you that job, God did. You do the very best you can and you watch patiently, God will promote you to a better place.

But if you don't stay faithful, He's going to let you wallow and stay in that misery, because you are better off staying there learning faithfulness than taking your unfaithfulness and impatience to the next level.

The Word says, "For in due season we shall reap, if we faint not" (Galatians 6:9). The Lord knew there were going to be seasons in your life. I call these seasons "in-between times." It's like when one door shuts, yet no other door has opened in front of you. The one door shuts, but there's still a closed door in front of you and you're thinking, "Do I go back from where I came? Or do I press forward?"

I like what my husband says, "You can't be past-possessed. You have to be forward-focused." You have to press forward. When you get your praise on, that gives you extra power to press forward. My praise is pressing on the door. Then my worship presses. Then my prayer presses some more. Suddenly, the door comes open.

It's easy to shout when we're coming out, it's easy to shout when we're going in. But what about those in-between times when we find ourselves in a lonely corridor with that artificial light and no open doors? It's hard to shout when our back is against one wall and our nose is against the other. It seems like there is no way out. That's the reason God says in the scripture you're going to become weary. You're going to become faint. You're going to feel like giving up. But He's also saying that if you just hang on and trust the Word that

He's given you, if you faint not, He promises that in due season, you will reap your reward. You will have what He promised you. But you cannot faint.

God knows the precise timing for everything in your life, for the fulfillment of everything in your life that He has promised you and prepared for you to live out in your lifetime. No one else can know that. You can't. Your pastor can't. Not even your closest friend. But God knows. Psalm 139 says, "You saw me before I was born. Every day of my life was recorded in your book. Every moment was laid out before a single day had passed" (Psalm 139:16).

Do you realize that before you were even conceived in your mother's womb, He knew all the promises He would have for you? He knew the path that you were going to take. He had already designed a special plan for you, and He also knew the path that you would choose to take. Sometimes we choose a road other than what He has prepared for us because we get anxious or impatient. We get weary and give into our weariness and begin to walk down a road that was not designed for us. Thank goodness God has a long arm, and a loving arm, and a caring heart that He can reach down and pick us up, and put us back on the right road.

Circumstance cannot determine what God has promised you. It's easy to think, "If I could just change my circumstance, then that would bring about what God has promised me." We try to make things different. We think,

"Well, if I could just get a new job, if I could just get a better car, if I could just have prettier clothes, if I could just have a bigger house, *then* I know things would be much better." But see, it's not the things in the material world that satisfy. It's not the possessions and the money that give you the contentment, peace, and joy you will have in the center of God's will. When God created you, He built a little, empty, void spot into you, and there's only one thing that can fill it—God Himself. Money can't fill it. Your lover can't fill it. Your children can't fill it. Your job can't fill it. Food can't fill it. Alcohol can't fill it. Nothing can fill it except God Himself.

Stop chasing after things in the natural world. Don't let your daily wants and desires distract you from the dream God has put in your heart. Even so, don't rush to make the big picture you see in your spirit happen too quickly; don't push God into moving faster—you can't force love. Stand firm in His Word; seek after God and His righteousness; seek after His Kingdom, His truth, His Spirit, and not only will you see your dream come to pass, everything else you need and want will be added to you as well.

Holy Spirit, thank you for refreshing me day by day. Help me to not grow weary, to not grow impatient or bitter, but to run my race in faith and to not faint. You alone I seek; only in Your Presence will I find fullness of joy. Thank You for being present with me every moment of everyday. That alone is all I desire.

One Minute of Praise

One Minute of Praise:

Take your mind off the frustrations of the day—the aching feeling of not moving forward, or perhaps not even knowing what direction forward might be. Focus on God's faithfulness and all you know He has planned for you in due season.

_____

_____

_____

_____

_____

_____

_____

_____

THIRTY-SIX

Praise-Worth Equals Self-Worth

And she [Leah] conceived again and bore a son, and said, This time I will praise the Lord. Therefore she called his name Judah.

Genesis 29:35

In the story of Leah and Jacob, we read that Leah was living in the shadow of Rachel. She was a victim of her circumstances. Even so, she was determined to make the best of an unfortunate situation. She thought to herself, "I'm going to do everything within my power to make my husband love me." Have you ever said to yourself, "I will make them be my friend. I will make this man love me. I will make my co-workers respect me."? You know what I'm talking about?

In that same way, Leah was determined in her heart to turn things around. When Jacob came in at the end of the day, all of his ironing had been done. His house had been cleaned. He didn't even have to carry the trash out because she had already carried it to the dumpster. When he got in, supper was prepared; and as he sat down to eat, she went out and polished the spokes of his chariot. She thought, "I've got to make him love me because he's my desire. He's what I want. He's my life." Then she thought, "I'll give him a baby, I know that will make him love me because nobody else has given him a child."

So, she conceived and brought forth a child by the name of Rueben. Back in those days, they would name their children according to what was happening in their life at that moment. Every name had a meaning. So she named the first child Rueben, which meant, "Look at me; see my affliction." She thought, "Surely, if you see the pain that I've gone through, you will love me." But the atmosphere in the house did not change. She thought, "If I give him two children, then he will love me." So she brought forth Simeon, which means "listen to me; hear me." In other words, "Do you not hear me crying out for your affection? Do you not hear my moans and groans at night yearning to be loved as your wife and not just as a woman to give you children—but to be heard and appreciated by you?"

Then she thought, "That didn't work. Maybe three. Maybe if I give him three children." So she conceived again and she gave birth to Levi. Levi means "to be joined together; to be connected." She thought, "Surely, after I give him three sons, I will be connected to him. I will be joined to him." But things still did not change. She was in one of those in-between times with her back against the wall and her nose against a shut door. She was still in a lonely, desperate season, but she was trying to move into a new season of love, comfort, and harmony. She was using her power to open the door and move out of that in-between place.

But something happened between child number three and child number four. I think God perhaps had a conversation with her.

Have you ever had one of those uncomfortable conversations? You feel like, "God, I really didn't want to hear this today." And He's saying, "Listen to Me, because I have a word for you. You're to be obedient and this is what you're supposed to do." And you're saying, "But God, I don't want to do that." Then He speaks to you and says, "Remember, it's not all about you."

I believe the Lord had a similar conversation with Leah. When she gave birth to a fourth child, she named the child

Judah: "I will praise Him." What changed? She was now saying, "I will praise my God—no matter what."

Did you know all the descendants of Judah through the generations were known as praisers? Do you realize what she gave birth to because her attitude and her focus changed? Do you have any idea what you can give birth to in the spiritual realm when you just begin to praise God without compromise?

Lord, what wisdom and mercy You have ordained that we should only need to praise You. Help us by Your Spirit to continually offer You praise, to have our self-worth tied to Your praises, to be resolutely determined to praise You without compromise—to be desperately addicted to praising You at all times!

One Minute of Praise:

What can we learn from Leah and the tribe of Judah? How can you begin to turn your circumstances around, one minute at a time?

_____

_____

_____

_____

THIRTY-SEVEN

Flow in the Current of Praise

Draw near to God and He will draw near to you.

James 4:8 NKJV

*J*once heard T.D. Jakes share this story about the Titanic. Why did so many people drown when there were enough lifeboats stowed on the ship to save everyone? What happened was when the ship went down, people filled the lifeboats—but because there was such a suction caused by the undercurrent surrounding the sinking ship, the lifeboats that were too close to the ship were sucked down with it. All those boats filled with people that didn't get far enough away from the sinking ship were sucked into its downward pull.

This illustrates why it is so important not to hang around negative people—negative people create a force around them just like a sinking ship—it can pull all the other boats down with it. If you don't know how to stay clear, you will be pulled under by the negative influences surrounding you. You've got to break some of those influences—some of which are in the form of relationships. If you're going to be a praiser, you've got to choose what you expose yourself to, including who you hang around. You've got to get away from those ships that are going down. If you don't, they will suck you under and you will become just like them. The words they speak will become your words. Their attitudes will become your attitudes. What they want in life will become what you want in life. You will find yourself forgetting that God has put a lion of Judah inside of you and you were designed and called to worship Him.

Don't become intimately associated with people who do not lift God up and glorify Him. You can minister to those people as God leads you, but they should not make up your inner circle of friends and confidantes. Guard your close relationships, as you do your heart, because you have been carefully designed for such a time as this. You have been set apart to be a worshipper. Don't let the influences of the world keep you from praising God through every situation. When people are ignoring you, praise Him anyhow.

When that promotion passes you by, praise Him anyhow. When you become older and your children have turned their back on you and don't call you anymore, praise Him anyhow. When you don't have anybody to help you pay your light bill, praise Him anyhow. When you get accused of something you've never done, just praise Him. When your body is so wracked with pain you're hurting in every joint—just praise Him. When there's no money to buy food and there's no food in the refrigerator, and you wonder, "God, what am I going to do?" Just praise God. When the company you've worked with for twenty-five years suddenly downsizes and cuts off your retirement and you wonder, "What am I going to do? I've given twenty-five years of my life to this company." Just praise Him. When your friends and your family don't understand your relationship and your walk with God—they don't understand when they hear you in the bathroom praising Him—they don't understand when you're walking out to the car with praise on your lips—they don't understand anything about all this praise, that's okay. Just praise Him because it's time to stop seeking man's approval and to focus on God's approval. You be approved by God and I promise you, people you need favor with in the world will have favor for you because God will set it up.

When you pray, God listens—but when you praise Him, He actually seeks after you. Did you get that? When I pray and I take my petitions to the Lord, He listens, but when I begin to worship Him, *He* comes for *me*. Draw near to God, and *He* will draw near to *you*.

> *God, as I leave today to go to work, I thank you for Your protection, I thank you for taking care of my kids at school—that You'll protect them and not let any harm come to them—I just want to give You glory for that protection. And Lord, I want to give You glory for the angels that You've assigned to watch over me. Thank you for all Your watchful care and affection toward me.*

One Minute of Praise:

You know what draws you near to God, and what draws God near. Take one minute to do that now.

_____

_____

_____

_____

_____

_____

_____

_____

_____

THIRTY-EIGHT

Strength through Praise

The thief does not come except to steal, and to kill, and to destroy.

John 10:10 NKJV

What's the difference between a thief and a robber? There's a major difference. To me, robbers are people who steal quickly—they are here and gone. They break a window and grab whatever they see. It could be totally valueless or worth thousands, but it is all chance. They just grab whatever they can get their hands on.

But let me tell you something about a thief. A thief strategizes. A thief watches when you come and when you go.

More than likely, they've even been in your home and have seen what you have. They have pinpointed the most valuable things and have begun planning how they will get away with taking them. They strategize for weeks, even months, before finally making their move. Then, when they do make their move, they go for your most valuable possessions.

Why does the Word say that Satan comes *as a thief* to kill, steal, and destroy? Do you know what the most valuable thing in your possession is? Your praise. Why do you think he doesn't want you to get your praise on? Why do you think he doesn't want that Judah residing in you to come forth? Because he knows if he can get your praise, then he has control of your victory. If he can get your praise, then he has your confidence. If he can get your praise, then he has your self-esteem. If he can get your praise, then he knows that he will eventually get control of your mind. If he can get your praise, then he will have control of your spirit. If he can get your praise, then he will have control of what you focus on. If he can get your praise, then he's going to have control of your ears and what you listen to. If he can get your praise, then he has control of what comes out of your mouth.

There are times when we take our petitions to the Lord, but there are also times when God says, "Stop backing your dump truck up and dumping all of your cares and your burdens on the floor of my court, and then loading them back up and taking them with you. I want your praise—leave that stuff at my feet and walk out singing a victory song!"

I know we're a needy people, but there are times when God doesn't need to hear anything more about our problems, because we've already told Him about them in intimate detail. It's all we talk about! He doesn't need to hear anything more about how sad your life is, how your husband has run off with your friend's wife, how your kids are hooked on cocaine and have dropped out of school. God isn't concerned as much with the problems as He is with your faith in Him as the Deliverer! He wants you to know that if you'll get your praise, then the other things are going to take care of themselves.

Thank you Lord for helping me to stay focused on You. I refuse to let the enemy steal my praise, my peace, and my joy. Holy Spirit, I invite You to prompt me when my gaze begins to be pulled away from the hope I have in Jesus. Remind me to take every thought captive and to think and speak only those things that are praiseworthy and pleasing to You.

One Minute of Praise:

Take one minute to fix your thoughts on what is true and honorable and right. Think about things that are pure and lovely and admirable—whatever is excellent and worthy of praise. Think on these things for the next minute—and let your praises flow.

THIRTY-NINE

Praise That Purifies; Praise That Prevails

You will tear all your enemies apart, making chaff of mountains. You will toss them in the air, and the wind will blow them all away; a whirlwind will scatter them. And the joy of the Lord will fill you to overflowing.

Isaiah 41:15,16

When you praise God, He rewards you with His presence. You may only have a minute now, then a minute at noon, and then a minute at three, and then a minute at five, and then a minute at seven, and a minute at nine, and a minute as you're going to bed at night. But do you realize that during all of those minutes, and throughout the times in between, His presence could be with you if you would just invite Him with your praise?

When you start praising Him—giving Him one minute of praise whenever you can—I promise you with every minute of praise you will be feeding the lion of Judah inside of you. When that lion of Judah rises up, you're enemy is going to flee for his life. You will be wielding that two-edge sword of His Word with confidence.

When you get your praise on, your blade is going to be so shiny that just the glare is going to blind the enemy— your sword is going to gleam because you've got your lathe of praise on full power. The Word filling your thoughts, and the Word spoken forth will strengthen your weapon. The enemy won't even be able to see where you are because of the light reflecting off of you.

Look at Isaiah 41:15,16 ESV:

Behold, I make of you a threshing sledge, new, sharp, and having teeth; you shall thresh the mountains and crush them, and you shall make the hills like chaff; you shall winnow them, and the wind shall carry them away, and the tempest shall scatter them. And you shall rejoice in the Lord; in the Holy One of Israel you shall glory.

What does the word "chaff" mean? We want victory in our life, but are we willing to go to the threshing floor? We want to be anointed—we want all of the benefits of being blessed—but are we willing to pay the price? Why is the threshing floor so important? After wheat is harvested and before it can be of any value, the chaff and the grain of wheat must be separated. It is only the wheat that gives us grain to make bread, flour to make cakes, and other components to make cereal. What does the wheat have to go through to be useable? It has to be separated from its protective covering—the chaff. It has to be crushed. It has to be put down on the threshing floor and sifted. During that process, the wheat is in transition—it's in one of those in-between times—like when your back's against the wall and you don't see any way out.

There's only one way you're going to make it. You've got to take yourself to the threshing floor. You've got to let God come down and sift you. Whatever the enemy has brought against you, you've got to let God begin to crush it, and crush it, and crush it. It's not comfortable. It's even painful. It hurts because many times it seems like the situation is just getting worse. You're asking God, "Shouldn't this season be over? Why is it taking so long? Your cry out, "Lord, I can't take it any more!"

If you listen, you'll hear God replying, "Be patient, when you are broken, sifted, and refined, I will send the wind of my Holy Spirit. When I blow upon you, all that will be left is grain. No impurities. No chaff. Pure grain that's perfect to make the bread I have created you to be." When God takes you to the threshing floor and you respond with praise saying, "God, I don't know how long I've got to stay in these in-between times, but I trust that You're going to bring me out because that's what Your Word says."

When you respond with a grateful attitude, let me tell you what's going to happen. What's been stored up with the wicked will be released to you, because the Word says it has been stored up for the righteous. Who are the righteous? It's those who have made God the center of their life. Has God given you a promise? Hang on to it just like Leah did. Don't you begin to walk around and say, "God, just listen to me. Oh Lord, I want to be connected to You. Oh Lord, I'm in so much pain." Instead say, "God, I don't care what happens to me. I don't care if I go down tomorrow. I don't care if I lose my house. I don't care if my husband walks out on me. I don't care if nobody talks to me again and it's just me and You. I will get my praise on. I will praise You anyhow."

You get your praise on in those in-between times—in those seasons when you're on the threshing floor—and in due season that door of provision will open up and you will walk on through to victory.

Lord, I know You are faithful and always with me. I thank you, Lord, for ordering my steps, working all things out for my good, and for preparing me and making me a vessel of Your honor. I will praise You at all times, knowing You are the author and the finisher of my faith. You have preordained every situation

and circumstance so that I would fulfill the purpose to which you have called me. I give You praise and glory and honor, even while here on the threshing floor.

One Minute of Praise:

Think about one of the "in-between" places in your life. With that in mind, praise the Lord.

_____

_____

_____

_____

IX.

The Transforming Power of A Grateful Heart

FORTY

Simple Gratitude

Then one of them, when he saw that he was healed, turned back, praising God with a loud voice; and he fell on his face at Jesus' feet, giving him thanks. Now he was a Samaritan. Then Jesus answered, "Were not ten cleansed? Where are the nine? Was no one found to return and give praise to God except this foreigner?" And he said to him, "Rise and go your way; your faith has made you well."

Luke 17:15-19 ESV

Not long ago, a dear friend of ours, Dr. Adrian Rogers, received his assignment to change locations. This mighty warrior of God made a powerful statement that will be etched in my memory forever. He said, "I would rather

 Simple Gratitude

stand alone in the light of truth, than in a crowd filled with error." What he was saying is, "I would rather live in a cave on a desolate island, or live anywhere alone in integrity, purity, and righteousness, than compromise my convictions just to receive the approval and applause of man. I would let everyone walk out of my life if it were the only way to remain honest, grateful, thoughtful, and thankful."

In the same way, we must guard our relationship with our Heavenly Father. The greater the anointing in your life, the more isolated you will become from the cares of this world. A desire to please your Heavenly Father will replace the desire to please your best friend. What do you possess that you can share with your Heavenly Father that will please Him the most?

A minister friend of mine, Dr. Pat Schatzline, President of Forerunner School of Ministry in Birmingham, Alabama, preached a sermon about "The Three Times Jesus Got Upset." The first time Dr. Pat mentioned was when Jesus entered the temple while they were having a party that he had not been invited to. The Pharisees had turned the Father's house into a den of thieves. He went through the temple turning tables over as the money exchanged for doves and other merchandise went flying through the air. These people had lost their respect and gratitude for the House of God.

The second time Dr. Pat described is found in Matthew 26:39-45. Jesus invited His disciples to spend one hour praying with Him. As he was praying, Oh Father let this cup pass from me, yet not my will, but Thine be done, His disciples fell asleep. He went a second time to pray, returned, and they had fallen asleep again. He went a third time to pray and once again, when He returned, He found them asleep. He asked, "Could you not spend one hour praying with me? For thirty-three years I have walked this earth and felt your pain. For three and a half years I have walked beside you and fed you. You have seen miracle after miracle and all I asked for was one hour."

If they would have only understood what was just ahead of them. Perhaps if they could have seen a few hundred feet into the black of the night as Judas waited in the shadows to betray the One they had disappointed by falling asleep, perhaps they would have remained watchful. It would have been easier to stay awake to pray, but the time to pray had passed and now it was too late.

The third group of people Dr. Pat talked about was the ten healed lepers. Why did only one out of ten lepers returned to tell Jesus "thank you"? The story in Luke 17:12-19, tells us Jesus was passing through Samaria and Galilee. When He entered a certain village, He was met by ten lepers. All ten shouted aloud, "Jesus, Master, have mercy on us!" He replied, "Go show yourselves unto the priests." The Word says as they went they were healed, but the story does not end there. The scripture says in verse fifteen that when one of them saw that he was healed, he turned back and with a loud voice glorified God. He fell down on his face at the feet of Jesus and gave thanks.

Jesus responded, "Were there not ten cleansed? Where are the nine?" The only one that came back was a foreigner—a Samaritan. He was not even from the seed of Abraham, Isaac, and Jacob. Why did he return and none of the other nine?

Could it have been that it is easy to take for granted the people who are the closest to us? The miraculous becomes the norm. The one from outside of his circle, outside of his house, outside of his city, was the only one who came back to say "thank you." May it not be so among us.

Father God, forgive me for taking Your goodness and grace for granted. Lord Jesus, help me to never lightly esteem all You've done for me through the cross. Holy Spirit, make me mindful every moment of Your presence in my life. I am so grateful for all I've been given in Christ—thank you for Your Word, Your Son, Your Name, and Your Spirit. Father God, Lord Jesus, and Holy Spirit, blessed Trinity, how I esteem and worship Your majesty, power, and glory forever.

One Minute of Praise:

Think of all that you have, all that you are, in Christ. What precious promises are available to you as a believer in Jesus? Meditate for just a minute—and give thanks—for all the Lord has provided to those who believe.

_____

_____

_____

_____

_____

_____

_____

_____

_____

FORTY-ONE

Gratitude Brings Wholeness

Give thanks in all circumstances, for this is God's will for you in Christ Jesus.

1 Thessalonians 5:18 NIV

Jesus' heart was broken when He walked into His Father's house and found it messed up by ungrateful people. His heart ached inside when His disciples could not even stay awake for one hour to pray with Him. Then we find Him in Luke asking the question, "Where are the other nine?"

184　　　　　　　　　One Minute of Praise

In Luke 17:17, Jesus is asking the leper from Samaria a very important question, "Were there not ten cleansed? But where are the nine?" The leper replies, "Lord, although I am but a Samaritan, I just had to come back and say 'thank you.'" Jesus answered with a powerful statement, "Arise, go thy way; thy faith has made thee whole." In verse fourteen we read, "As they went on their way they were healed," but in verse nineteen it states, "the one that returned was made whole."

Let's talk about the word *whole*. Jesus said, "Thy faith has made thee *whole*." We can define the word *whole* as meaning "complete, total, in one piece, intact, unharmed, undamaged." Some translations of the Bible use the word *well*. The word *well* can be defined as "healthy, fine, glowing, vigorous, and strong." The leper's thankful heart delivered him from his past mistakes and all the penalties that resulted. The one leper that returned received something more than the nine that chose not to return. The nine were healed, but the tenth was made in every way *whole* and *complete*.

As he returned to say "thank you," do you think it was possible that his fingers began to grow back and his hair returned? Can you see the picture at the next lepers' anonymous meeting—the other nine lepers are holding cups of coffee with their nubs when they meet up with leper number ten who's holding his cup with ten fingers? Then they glance up and see his curly, raven black hair flowing down beside his perfectly sculpted face. Now there's a picture!

I heard the other day that Charles Brown gives nine reasons why only one leper returned to say "thank you" to Jesus:

1. One waited to see if the cure was real.

2. Another waited to see if it would last.

3. The third would tell Jesus "thank you" later on.

4. The fourth felt he'd never had leprosy in the first place.

5. The fifth figured he would have gotten well anyway.

6. The sixth said, "The priest did it for me, I gave glory to the priest."

7. The seventh thought, "Jesus really didn't do anything. He just looked at us."

8. The next to last said, "Any rabbi could have done that."

9. The ninth commented, "I was already getting better."

Do you consider your heart thankful or unthankful? Take this test.

Ten ways of knowing if you have a thankful heart:

1. Praise comes easy to you. You don't have to be prompted to give thanks.

2. You desire to change a person's opinion through showing compassion and kindness.

3. You look for ways to bless others.

One Minute of Praise

4. Your testimony is not a past memory, but the way you start every conversation.

5. People want to bless you because they see your grateful heart.

6. You live your life seeing miracles.

7. You are ever thankful for God's mercy toward you.

8. You don't judge other people because you know from where you have come.

9. You beg God for a chance to share what you have been given.

10. You exemplify a lifestyle of forgiveness.

If you are looking to justify why you live with an ungrateful heart, there are plenty of reasons you can come up with. It could be what someone did to you when you were a child. Perhaps what a former employer said to you. Maybe it was your spouse that walked out on you. The list could go on and on, but in every case you lose. You try to ease your pain by going through life justifying your attitude. You try to get even with those who have hurt you, but nothing you do or say eases the pain. The hurt only grows. The answer is not in getting even, but in forgiving because you are grateful for Jesus forgiving you.

The only person that you should want to even the score with is the one who has blessed you. This will change who you are and the way you think. A thankful attitude will melt

 Gratitude Brings Wholeness

a bitter person's heart. An attitude of gratitude turned Scrooge into a cheerful giving man on Christmas morning. A grateful heart transforms a self-centered Grinch into someone who tells his dog Rex, "I love you."

There are over 3,000 references to "thanksgiving" in the Bible. Take a minute right now to express your heartfelt gratitude to God your Father for something He has done for you. God is drawn to your words of thanks and praise. "Oh, give thanks to the Lord of lords! For His mercy endures forever" (Psalm 136:3 NKJV). When you say "thank you," God's love flows freely. It goes on forever and ever. He will chase after you from the time you get up in the morning until you go to bed at night. Just think, it only takes two small but powerful words to find favor with the King: "Thank you!"

Thank You Lord God for Your Word! Thank you for Your goodness and mercy! Thank you for Your steadfast love and faithfulness! Thank you for the hope I have in You. Thank you for Your creation! Thank you that I am wonderfully and fearfully made! Thank you!

One Minute of Praise:

How many things can you think of to be thankful for? Express them to God right now—for one minute.

One Minute of Praise

FORTY-TWO

Mindful of Favor

O God, you are my God; earnestly I seek you; my soul thirsts for you; my flesh faints for you, as in a dry and weary land where there is no water. So I have looked upon you in the sanctuary, beholding your power and glory. Because your steadfast love is better than life, my lips will praise you. So I will bless you as long as I live; in your name I will lift up my hands.

Psalm 63:1-4 ESV

One Sunday morning as I sat on the platform during our worship service, my eyes could not help but focus on a young man by the name of Brian A. Brian A. was just released from jail. Bryan B., whose family is a member of our church, was arrested for attempted murder. While in jail, Bryan B. recommitted his life to the Lord and began to lead other inmates to Christ. Brian A. was his cell mate and not only did Brian A. give his life to the Lord in his jail cell, but he was filled with the Holy Spirit with the evidence of speaking in tongues. The Holy Spirit was so new to him; he was not even sure what he had received. He just knew he felt something inside that he had never felt before and it felt good. He said, "I feel forgiven and all clean inside."

I watched intensely as this young man, just released from jail three days prior, now wept through the entire service with his hands raised up over his head and his wife, whom he had led to the Lord, stood worshipping next to him. He had been saved, filled with the Holy Spirit, brought his wife into the Kingdom, and now here he was, standing in our church service with his arms and hands as high as they could stretch. And to think, prior to three days ago, he was behind bars with no hope, freedom, or gratitude. What had changed?

Someone greater than you and I had been introduced to Brian A. This Person had forgiven him of his wrongdoings. This Person had healed his broken heart. This Person by the name of Jesus Christ had given him a future and erased his past. He now had hope, freedom, and new life. He was so grateful for someone who believed in him, who did not let his past mistakes hinder their relationship.

All through praise and worship and the preaching of the Word, all Brian could do was weep. The glow upon his face betrayed all that was happening in his heart.

What was the difference between Brian and a young man three rows back that comes to church, stands during worship service with his hands in his pockets and maybe sings only one or two stanzas of a song before he decides to sit down? Could it be the young man three rows back had forgotten from where he has come? Revelations 2:5 tells us that when we forget from where God has brought us, we need to do the first works over. In other words, Jesus is saying; "Repent and ask Me to forgive you for being ungrateful and self-centered." The Lord will do just that. You will once again find that first love and have a desire to worship him just like Brian A. Gratitude, thankfulness, and appreciation for the One who has given you air to breath, wisdom, strength, and a freedom to worship will come voluntarily from your heart.

Webster's dictionary defines *thanks* as "mindful or aware of favor." Can you say "thank you" for what God brought you through a month ago? It's easy to be thankful for the good times in life, but what about the not so pleasant times in life that revealed the perfect plan of God to get you where you need to be in Him? You had to walk to work before God blessed you with a car. You had your utilities turned off and lived in the dark a few days and now when you flip the light switch on you cannot help but give Him praise. Perhaps you didn't have enough money to buy food for your family and now you understand that the Lord was teaching you the importance of giving thanks before you ate the food placed on your table.

Mindful of Favor

191

It's not easy talking about the tough times in life, but I believe it is the tough times in life that set us up for the blessing waiting to be released to a grateful heart. I owe Him everything I have, what about you? Of the 1,440 minutes you have in a day, could you not give Him one? Could you not give Him one minute of praise and thanksgiving for how far He has brought you from the difficulties of your past?

Thank you Father God for all You have done for me over the course of my life. Forgive me for being neglectful, prideful, selfish, and ungrateful. You are everything to me—without You, I am nothing. You are my Rock, my Strong Tower, and my salvation. Your are my peace, my joy, and my strength. All my hope is in You. I love You and worship You, and give You thanks.

One Minute of Praise:

Where has God brought you? Can you think of anything to be grateful for? Express it to God now—for one minute.

_____

_____

_____

_____

One Minute of Praise

FORTY-THREE

Givers and Takers

I will give to the Lord the thanks due to his right-eousness, and I will sing praise to the name of the Lord, the Most High.

Psalm 7:17 ESV

M an was created in the beginning to be a giver. He gave names to the animals in the garden. He gave his rib to Eve. But after Adam ate of the forbidden fruit, the generations who followed became takers. A taker always wants something that a giver can only get. What man once had ownership of had now been taken away. As long as he was a giver, he enjoyed daily strolls through the garden walking and talking with his Father, but when he chose to be a taker, his privileges were removed.

 Givers and Takers

Let us look at heaven's former worship leader, Lucifer. He was created and given the power within him to move through Heaven and usher Heaven into worship. But when he wanted more, becoming a taker, he lost everything.

In both cases, as long as they were givers, Adam and Lucifer both possessed a precious gift that only a giver is privileged to have, but when their lust for more rose above their desire to bless, the only thing they were left with was an unquenchable thirst to possess what only givers can have. Only by God's grace can we truly change from a taker to a giver.

The Bible is filled with takers and givers. The first king of Israel, Saul, once a mighty anointed man of God, disobeyed God and lived the rest of his life tormented with an evil spirit (See 1 Samuel 16:14). Jacob stole Esau's birthright and that blessing caused Jacob to fear for his life, because Esau wanted to kill him. Jacob lost the people he loved due to his deceitful, selfish spirit (See Genesis 27). In John 6:9-13, we find the little lad with five loaves of bread and two small fish. He gave all that he had and look what happened. His unselfish gesture fed five thousand and filled twelve baskets with leftovers. Look at Abraham in Genesis 22. Because of Abraham's obedience to give his son Isaac as a sacrifice, God provided His Son for the salvation of all! The Word says in Genesis 22:16-17,

> *This is what the Lords says: Because you have obeyed me and have not withheld even your*

beloved son, I swear by my own self that I will bless you richly. I will multiply your descendants into countless millions, like the stars of the sky and the sand on the seashore. They will conquer their enemies, and through your descendants, all the nations of the earth will be blessed—all because you have obeyed Me."

Everyday when you get up, warfare begins inside of you between your flesh man (a taker) and your spirit man (a giver). What you release from your mouth will determine which man will rise over the other. Will your life be filled with dreams, visions, and desires, but never go beyond where you are? Or will your dreams, visions, and desires become a reality because your spirit man rules your life? Will you choose to go through life wanting something that you can never have? It is the difference between being a taker and a giver. The choice is yours.

When was the last time you got out of bed and danced before the Lord and said "thank you?" At the age of eighty-eight, Smith Wigglesworth danced before the Lord as the words "thank you" leapt from his lips.

Listen to these words found in the book of Psalms:

I will thank you in front of the entire congregation. I will praise you before all the people.

Givers and Takers

Enter his courts with thanksgiving; go into his courts with praise.

Psalms 100:4

I will thank the Lord because he is just; I will sing praise to the name of the Lord Most High.

Psalms 7:17

In Daniel 6:10, we read about King Darius establishing a decree and signing the law stating that if any one ask a petition of any god for thirty days, he shall be cast into a den of lions. When he heard, Daniel went into his house, opened his windows facing Jerusalem, and knelt upon his knees three times a day not only to pray but also to give thanks before his God. He thanked his God in front of the entire city, including the officials and princes of the land. After these men witnessed Daniel praying and giving thanks to God, they sentenced him to death. Daniel knowingly gave up his life in order to say "thank you" to his Heavenly Father. When was the last time you got in trouble for saying "thank you"?

The story doesn't end there, though. Because Daniel had touched the heart of God with his gratitude, God turned those meat-eating lions into vegetarians for the night.

When trouble comes your way, when the enemy sets a trap to trick you into discouragement, anger, or depression,

God can turn what was supposed to destroy you into a pillow to sleep. Be a thanks giver! A grateful heart not only satisfies your soul, it can save your life.

Today I choose to be a giver, but most importantly, to be a thanks giver. Thank You Lord for Who You are and all You have done for me. Help me to remain thankful throughout the day and be a witness of Your goodness and grace. Help me to silence my enemies and bring You glory by keeping an attitude of gratitude at all times.

One Minute of Praise:

You can do all things through Christ, even give thanks! Because all things are possible to those who believe, you can remain grateful even in the most difficult situations. Give thanks!

FORTY-FOUR

What's the Password?

Make a joyful noise to the Lord, all the earth! Serve the Lord with gladness! Come into his presence with singing! Enter his gates with thanksgiving, and his courts with praise!

Psalm 100:1,2,4 ESV

*D*oes your computer talk to you? Mine does. It says things like, "Invalid password: Please re-enter." Whether I'm trying to retrieve my e-mail, check my bank balance, or pay a bill on line, it tells me I must have a password to enter my account. I type in every word and number that I can imagine, and the computer still says, "Invalid password."

Internet security advises me to use a different password for each of my logins. They suggest to occasionally change my password. How am I suppose to remember sixteen different passwords when I can't even remember one? Not to mention changing them every six months and putting them in a "secure place?" Now I've got to not only remember the password, but also the "secure place." I have undergone total frustration, hollered at my computer, wanted to kick it, and finally given up and made the time consuming phone calls to access my information. Then there I am, talking to a computer over the phone. "Press 1, press 4, press *," finally I give up and press 0 "to speak with a service representative." After being put on hold for ten minutes, I am finally allowed to speak with a genuine person. Then I hear these words: "Before I can access your account I will need to ask you a few questions. What's your mother's maiden name?" I am able to answer that. Next, "Where did your husband go to high school?" I can even answer that one. Finally the last question, "What is your pet's name?" Pet's name? I don't have a pet. Then you hear the voice on the other end of the line say, "I'm sorry, but unless you can tell me your pet's name we can not give you any information about this account."

I have been at my computer for two hours and haven't accomplished a thing, except being told, "Invalid password," and now I need to know the name of a pet that I don't have. Have you ever been there?

 What's the Password?

One afternoon as I sat at my computer, burying my head in my hands in complete frustration, the Holy Spirit spoke to me and said, "Your entry to Heaven's throne room has only one password and it never changes."

I said, "What did You say?"

Again He said, "Your entry to Heaven's throne room has only one password and it never changes. Once you know it, you have unlimited access. Unlimited access means access all day, all night, holidays, and weekends."

"What's the password, Lord?" I asked.

I grabbed my Bible, turned to the Old Testament, and there my eyes fell on Psalm 100:4: "Enter into His courts with praise."

"It's praise, Lord, it's praise!" I shouted. It's my praise that permits me to go into the presence of the King and have total access to His favor. It's all accessed by my praise.

When you create an atmosphere of praise, the Lord will move right in with you and smooth your way into or out of any situation. As long as you know the password, you have complete and total access to His presence anytime, anywhere.

My husband Randel has a desk drawer in his church office filled with nothing but candy. This candy is reserved for the children in the church who crawl up into his lap, hug his neck—not with a little squeeze, but a bear hug—and tell him how much they love him. They stretch their arms out and say, "Pastor I love you this much." He will ask, "How much?" And they stretch as far as they possibly can and say with a loud voice, "This much, a billion!" He will then say, "Okay, you can have one piece."

They'll jump down, knowing where the drawer is, open the drawer, stand there studying each piece of candy like they have never looked in the drawer before, and finally pick their favorite one and run out the door. Then their parent says, "Did you forget something?" "Oh yeah," they say. They run back to the pastor, hug his neck and say, "Thank you!" Then they'll charge out the office as if they had been given a million dollars.

Their pastor had the resources they wanted. The candy was there all the time waiting on them. They knew where it was, how to open the drawer, and what they were going to find in that drawer, but they had to know the password to gain access to that special drawer. They didn't become the recipient to the Pastor's resources until they used the password; a hug and "I love you." They almost forget one important element for re-entry and that was to say, "Thank you."

How much more important is it for us to show gratitude to our Heavenly Father for the things He has done for us? He's attracted to our praise, but He adores our "Thank yous."

I want you to know the Throne Room is filled with drawers just waiting to be accessed by you, drawers filled with:

 What's the Password? 201

- Finances: *"Beloved, I pray that you may **prosper** in all things and be in health, just as your soul prospers"* (3 John 2 NKJV).

- Blessings: *"The godly are showered with **blessings**"* (Proverbs 10:6).

- Healing: *"With his stripes we are **healed**"* (Isaiah 53:5 KJV).

- Restoration: *"And I will **restore** to you the years that the locust hath eaten"* (Joel 2:25 KJV).

- Confidence: *"Being **confident** of this very thing, that he which hath begun a good work in you will perform it until the day of Jesus Christ"* (Philippians 1:6 KJV).

- Strength: *"My grace is sufficient for thee: for my **strength** is made perfect in weakness"* (2 Corinthians 12:9 KJV).

- Wisdom: *"If any of you lacks **wisdom**, he should ask God, who gives generously to all without finding fault"* (James 1:5-6 NIV).

But to gain access you must use the password. God has given us the password to access His Throne and all of His promises through His Word. Your access will never be denied if you enter the correct password. "Enter...into His courts with praise!" (See Psalms 100:4 KJV.)

I will enter Your gates with thanksgiving in my heart, I will enter Your courts with praise! I will say this is the day that You have made! I will rejoice for You have made me glad!

One Minute of Praise:

Is there a drawer in the Lord's desk you would like opened to you? You know the password! Practice using it right now—for one minute.

_____

_____

_____

_____

_____

_____

_____

What's the Password?

FORTY-FIVE

Cultivating Grace and Favor

When Esther was taken to King Xerxes at the royal palace in early winter of the seventh year of his reign, the king loved her more than any of the other young women. He was so delighted with her that he set the royal crown on her head and declared her queen instead of Vashti.

Esther 2:16,17

The Old Testament tells us a story of a peasant girl named Esther. Esther understood the importance of knowing the password to gain access to the throne room.

One Minute of Praise

She had an understanding of her purpose in finding favor with the king. She had tapped into the resources to access favor. So why was a peasant girl from a nation in exile chosen as queen by a powerful Persian king?

Tommy Tenney says it so well in his book, *Finding Favor with the King*. He writes, "Who knows what can happen in your life when preparation intersects with protocol and destiny is birthed?"[9]

Esther not only had physical beauty, but she was clever. King Xerxes was attracted to Esther in an exceptional way that enticed him to desire her as his wife. She could have remained a concubine or a secondary wife, but she had become irresistible to him. What did she possess that the other women did not? What was her secret?

Could it have been that Esther knew the password to get her from where she was to the divine appointment that would change the history of a nation? She sought wisdom from the Lord about the moment in time she would need to seize to fulfill her destiny. She spent twelve months preparing for one encounter. The Bible says Esther spent the first six months of her stay in the king's palace undergoing a regimen involving oil of myrrh, followed by six months with special perfumes and ointments. Myrrh was used in the holy preparation of worship and ministry to God in the tabernacle of Moses. It was also burned before the Lord as holy incense. Before Esther had the special perfumes and ointments mas-

Cultivating Grace and Favor

saged into her skin, she had to be cleansed by oil of myrrh. Her preparation consisted of cleansing and purification of all toxins from both within and without. The constant bathing and application with oil of myrrh cleansed, purified, and softened the skin. When all the toxins were removed from her body she then received a beauty treatment of sweet smelling perfumes and ointments. The skin absorbed the fragrance so deeply that wherever she walked her fragrance announced her appearance before she arrived.

Esther was separated from her family, living with strangers, and competing with over fourteen hundred other women in preparation to be in the presence of the King for one night. Her desire to please the King was priority. Her preparation for King Xerxes became the norm, not the exception. It was a course of action that became her pleasure to pursue, not simply an obligatory routine. I believe she had fallen in love with the King, while all the other young girls had fallen in love with the kingdom and the life of luxury they could live as queen.

If your heart desires to find favor with the true King, you must:

1. **Purify yourself:** Purify yourself of any unclean, unholy thing that would prevent the King from desiring to spend time with you. The Word says: *"Purify me from my sins, and I will be clean; wash me, and I will be whiter than snow"* (Psalm 51:7).

2. **Call upon the Lord**: Prepare yourself by calling upon the Lord. Ask the Lord to remove anything within you that would hinder a visitation from Him. *"For whosoever shall call upon the name of the Lord shall be saved"* (Romans 10:13 KJV).

3. **Believe**: You must believe in your heart. *"Those who believe and are baptized will be saved. But those who refuse to believe will be condemned"* (Mark 16:16 TLB).

You are now ready to use the password that will give you access to the King. Esther 2:16 tells us that when Esther was taken to King Xerxes at the royal palace, the king loved her more than any of the other young women. He was so delighted with her that he set the royal crown on her head and declared her queen. If we could ask Esther, "Was all the preparation worth it?" What do you think she would say?

As I approach my King I want Him to be as delighted with me as King Xerxes was with Esther when he placed the royal crown upon her head and called her queen. I desire King Jesus to place His anointing upon my head and call me His beloved.

Holy Spirit, help me prepare myself to be pleasing before my King! Teach me how to cleanse and purify myself before the Lord and offer myself a living sacrifice to His Majesty. You, my Lord, are my only King, my truest desire, and deepest love, show me

how to enter Your Presence and obtain Your grace and favor. I praise and worship You, Lord, and offer You a thankful heart.

One Minute of Praise:

Invest the next sixty seconds in preparing yourself to enter the presence of the King of Kings.

FORTY-SIX

Praise in the Presence of Your Enemy

Thou preparest a table before me in the presence of mine enemies: thou anointest my head with oil; my cup runneth over. Surely goodness and mercy shall follow me all the days of my life: and I will dwell in the house of the Lord for ever.

Psalm 23:5-6 KJV

When Tommy Tenney preached a sermon in our church last fall called "Queen Esther," he told the story of how Queen Esther put her life in jeopardy by going before the king uninvited. She knew if he chose not to raise the gold scepter before her, she would die. But her trust was not in man, it was in the Lord. As she approached the king, he did raise the gold scepter, welcoming her into his court.

She stepped forward touching the tip of the gold scepter as he asked, "What do you want, Queen Esther? What is your request? I will give it to you, even if it is half the kingdom!"

She replied, "If it please Your Majesty, let the king and Haman come today to a banquet I have prepared for the king."

The king had offered her half the kingdom, and all she wanted was to prepare him a banquet and even invite her enemy, Haman! What was she thinking? I like how Mr. Tenney explained it, "If your enemy is the King's enemy, then your battle is the King's battle." She knew the battle was not hers, but it belonged to the Lord.

When you find favor with the King, you can ask anything in His name and he will do it. (See John 14:14.) When you find favor with the King, you can call upon Him and you will be saved from your enemies. (See Psalm 18:3.) When you find favor with the King, no weapon formed against you will prosper. (See Isaiah 54:17.)

Esther began to plan the menu for the banquet. She knew the importance of preparation. She had spent one year preparing for favor. "What should she feed the King?" Perhaps she knew the way to a man's heart is through his stomach! The menu was certainly a high priority. After all, she was his wife and above all else wanted to please Him, even before her desire to seek his favor. I believe God enjoys seeing our heart desiring to please him more than desiring His favor.

She did not allow the presence of Haman to distract her. What do you do when you feel your enemy advancing until he's in your court and even sitting at your table? Do you prepare a private party of praise, invite the King and ask the enemy to be your special guest? The Word says in Acts 16:18 that Paul commanded, "In the name of Jesus Christ come out" and when he spoke those words the enemy instantly left. Esther's enemy had already been defeated. She just needed to walk in the steps that had been ordered by God and leave the rest up to the Lord.

While Esther, King Xerxes, and Haman were dining at the banquet she had prepared, the king once again asked Esther, "Tell me what you really want." She replied, "I want to have another banquet tomorrow. I request your presence and also Haman's. Then tomorrow I will explain what this is about." Haman was a happy man! Little did Haman know that his presence in the palace did not affect her presence with the king.

When your praise welcomes the presence of the King, your enemy's presence will not affect your circumstance, your day, your situation, your conditions around you, or your presence with Him.

The food was on the table waiting for the arrival of King Xerxes and Haman. Once again King Xerxes asked the question, "Tell me what you want, even if it is half the kingdom." This time she responded, "If Your Majesty is pleased with me and wants to grant my request, my petition is that my life and the lives of my people will be spared." She explained how they had been sold as slaves and would be killed. The king replied, "Who would dare touch you?" I imagine at this moment Haman's heart was in the pit of his stomach. He knew what was about to unfold and what the end result would be.

Satan knows what his end result will be. He will try every trick in the book to distract, discourage, and defeat you. He knows the power that is in your praise. That is the reason he wants depression to come upon you, your kids strung out on drugs, cancer to attack your body, your mate to have an affair, because he knows if he can get your praise he will have your destiny. He knows that praise is the weapon that will ultimately destroy him. He also knows the end results of his kingdom; he will be locked in Hell for all eternity. Why be fearful of someone who has no favor with the King and has already been conquered at Calvary?

Esther now replies, "The wicked Haman is our enemy." The Word says, "Haman grew pale" (Esther 7:6 NIV). I believe at this point, Haman knew his fate; no different than our enemy knows his fate. He just needs to be reminded. The gallows that Haman had set up to hang Mordecai, Esther's uncle, became his own place of execution instead. The table Esther had prepared in the presence of her enemy took him down. Not only does the Lord prepare a table for you in the presence of your enemy, but He also invites you to sit at His right hand and He makes your enemy your foot-stool. (See Psalm 110:1.)

Esther gave all her attention to the king in the presence of her enemy. She ignored her enemy and pleased the king. The king's love for her protected and sheltered her allowing no harm to come upon her or her people. Praise in the midst of your enemy becomes his very own gas chamber. Your King's love for you will protect and shelter you allowing no harm to come upon you.

Esther's password to access the presence of the King was to first purify herself and approach him with praise and honor. She was then granted an audience with the king. If you want an audience with the King, purify yourself, brag on Him, and favor will be granted.

Lord, oh Lord, how excellent is Your Name in all the earth! You alone are worthy of my praise! I exalt You! I rejoice and declare, "This is the day that the Lord has made!" Yes! I will rejoice and be glad! You have prepared a table before me in the presence of

my enemies—You have defeated my every foe! I will praise You with every breath and with all my strength! No weapon formed against me shall prosper because You are my God! Praise You Lord for You reign in the earth, You reign in this day, and most of all, You reign in my heart!

One Minute of Praise:

Take a minute to set the table the Lord has prepared in the presence of your enemy!

One Minute of Praise

X.

Empowered, Equipped, and Elevated

FORTY-SEVEN

Extreme Praise

Praise the Lord! Praise God in his sanctuary; praise him in his mighty heavens! Praise him for his mighty deeds; praise him according to his excellent greatness!

Praise him with trumpet sound; praise him with the lute and harp! Praise him with tambourine and dance; praise him with strings and pipe! Praise him with sounding cymbals; praise him with clashing cymbals!

Let everything that has breath praise the Lord! Praise the Lord!

Psalm 150:1-6 ESV

God finds your extreme praise irresistible. What do I mean by extreme? Extreme praise refers to those

216 One Minute of Praise

powerful expressions of love to an ever-loving God that transcend admiration. It's a supernatural way to express the awesomeness of who He is. Are you ready to take your praise up a notch? Get ready; you will never be the same.

Extreme praise is a covenant connector between you and God. Extreme praise spoken through your lips will prepare your heart for an incredible manifestation of God's purpose and plan. Extreme praise will usher you into what you need to fulfill your purpose. Extreme praise allows you to become a vessel filled with God's presence. The only way you can get to the place of becoming a carrier of the anointing is to fix your thoughts upon the Lord. (See Isaiah 26:3.) Philippians 4:8 TLB states,

> Fix your thoughts on what is true and good and right. Think about things that are pure and lovely, and dwell on the fine, good things in others. Think about all you can praise God for and be glad about.

Fixing your thoughts means to give Him what He is worthy of. How do you *fix your thoughts?* You guard your eyes from unclean sight. You guard your ears from verbal garbage. You allow only good things to occupy your mind or come out of your mouth.

God wants to mold and shape you into a person of strong character worthy of His presence. It is constant work. It is a constant process of transformation. Once you

Extreme Praise

have a full understanding of the power that accompanies extreme praise, you will begin to experience more power and a greater anointing than you've ever had before.

Make the most of every opportunity to become the vessel of extreme honor that God has prepared you to be. Fill your thoughts and words with the extreme righteousness of God. When you offer up your praises, are they new every morning, or have they become routine? Extravagant praise is good. Extravagant praise brings extravagant results—and that's good—but extreme praise invades hell and exhilarates heaven! Become an extremist! Offer God the extreme praises worthy of His extreme love!

Thank you, Lord, for Your transforming power working in me as I praise You without reserve—for changing me from glory to glory as my praise for You becomes more extreme day by day. Expand my awareness of Your extreme goodness and mercy! Teach me to walk in the way of Your extreme grace and faithfulness. Help me to embrace and be a vessel of Your extreme love! Most of all, help me to love You more extremely.

One Minute of Praise:

Focus your mind on the extremity of God's grace and offer an extreme response—for the next sixty seconds.

_____

_____

_____

_____

_____

_____

_____

_____

FORTY-EIGHT

Praise Versus Worship

I will extol you, my God and King, and bless your name forever and ever. Everyday I will bless you and praise your name forever and ever. Great is the Lord, and greatly to be praised, and his greatness is unsearchable.

Psalm 145:1-3 ESV

There is more than one way to praise the Lord—and each act of praise can take you to a greater dimension of His presence.

Praise and worship, though closely related, need to be understood separately in order to appreciate more fully the true value of praise versus that of worship. Fuchsia Picket writes in her book, *Worship Him:*

Praise is one aspect of the worship experience for which the Scriptures give specific instructions regarding its place, purpose and power in our lives as worshippers.... Praise and thanksgiving dwell on the things God has done, is doing and is going to do, while worship expresses our devotion to God for who He is. Praising God brings us into His Presence and worship is our heart's response to God after we are in His Presence.[3]

Marcyne Heinrichs gives some great examples of how praise contrasts to worship:

Praise enjoys God; worship esteems Him.

Praise acclaims Him; worship beholds Him.

Praise lifts; worship bows.

Praise lauds, worship loves.

Praise celebrates; worship humbly reveres.

Praise addresses God; worship waits on God.

Praise dances; worship removes shoes for holy ground.

Praise extols God for what He's done; worship extols Him for who He is.

Praise Versus Worship

Praise says, "Praise the Lord"; worship demonstrates that "He is Lord."

Praise is grateful for heirship to the throne; worship lays crowns at His feet.[4]

You may ask the question, "I understand the power that is in my praise, but how do I get there? What catches the special attention of God? Are there more ways to praising God than just with my lips?"

The Hebrew language uses seven different words to refer to praise. Each has a somewhat different meaning which helps us to understand the many perspectives of praise:

Towdah refers to the offering of a sacrifice of praise and thanksgiving to honor God.

Yadah means "to praise by raising and extending the hands unashamedly unto God."

Zamar means "to touch the strings of a musical instrument."

Tehillah is a word translated as "song"—or "a song of praise."

Halal is the primary root in Hebrew for the universal praise word, "Hallelujah." It means "to shine, celebrate and rejoice in the Lord with a distinct sound."

Barak refers to blessing God as an act of adoration, kneeling expectantly and quietly before Him.

Shabach means "to address in a loud tone; to shout."

Praise that captures the attention of God can be vocal and physical, melodious and verbal, emotional and devotional. As you obey the command to praise God whether it be singing in the shower in the morning, shouting Hallelujah as you are trying to keep your cool driving to work, or just bragging on God for who He is as you wait for the traffic light to turn green; your praise summons the Holy Sprit to go before you, annihilating your enemy, and directing your path. What better way to begin your day, than being directed by the Holy Spirit as He walks one step ahead of you preparing the way?

Father, help me to exercise all the facets of praise You have ordained in Your Word. I know that as I apply these various elements of praise that You will inhabit each moment I focus my attention on You. Help me, Holy Spirit, to lift my intention, to attend my heart and mind more fully on heaven, and to be a vessel of Your Life here in the present.

One Minute of Praise:

How can you bring more aspects of praise into your daily experience? What are the little things you can do at seemingly inconsequential times that will create eternal, and even monumental results in your life now? Practice one of the forms of praise listed above for the next sixty seconds.

_____

_____

_____

_____

_____

_____

_____

One Minute of Praise

FORTY-NINE

Praise through Hard Times

About midnight Paul and Silas were praying and singing hymns to God, and the prisoners were listening to them, and suddenly there was a great earthquake, so that the foundations of the prison were shaken. And immediately all the doors were opened, ad everyone's bonds were unfastened.

Acts 16:25,26 ESV

*P*aul and Silas were stripped, beaten, and placed in stocks in the inner cell of a dark prison. Despite this depressing situation, they praised God, praying and singing praises as the other prisoners listened. Their praise dictated to their circumstance, not the other way around. The circumstance they were in had no authority over them because of their praise.

In Acts 16:26-34 we read, "There was a sudden earthquake and the doors flew open and the chains of every prisoner fell off." The chains of every prisoner literally fell right off! Not only did their praise profit them, but also the people around them.

When the jailer woke up and saw the prison doors wide open, he assumed the prisoners had escaped, so he drew his sword to kill himself. Paul shouted to him, "Don't do it! We are all here!" The story continues with the jailer calling for lights, running to the dungeon and falling down before Paul and Silas. He asks, "What must I do to be saved?" Not only did he get saved, but immediately went home and led everyone in his household to the Lord.

Because Paul and Silas chose to pursue praise above wallowing in their circumstance, not only did their praise silence their enemy and set them free, but an entire family came to know Christ.

Praise is powerful when understood and practiced. It's the difference between victory and defeat. The reason we praise God is to bring us into the presence of God—because it is in His presence we find fullness, completeness, power, authority, protection, shelter, refuge, strength, guidance, wisdom, understanding, and much more. And all we have to do is brag on God! I like what 2 Chronicles 20:15 KJV says, "Be not afraid nor dismayed by reason of this great multitude; for the battle is not yours, but God's."

I believe Job had to stand on those very words. Can you imagine how Job must have felt when he received word from his messengers that all his livestock, his servants, his sons and his daughters had perished in a single day? His wife's advice to him was to curse God and die. Now that's called "having a bad day." But we learn where Job's faith was through all of this in Job 1:21-22: "'I came naked from my mother's womb, and I will be stripped of everything when I die. The Lord gave me everything I had, and the Lord has taken it away. Praise the name of the Lord!' In all of this, Job did not sin by blaming God." Only a trusting heart will allow praise to fill your mouth when circumstances have pushed you to the breaking point.

When you feel overwhelmed by what is going on around you and you don't understand the "whys" or "what fors" of what is happening in your life—you must reaffirm your faith in God by striving for a deeper understanding of who He is. Get a fresh revelation of the greatness of God by meditating on the stories of faith and praise recorded in the Bible. Praising God for His goodness and greatness is the best way to renew your faith in Him.

Thank you Lord for Your faithfulness to me. I know Your Word will never fail me if I trust in You with my whole heart. Help me to lean not on my own understanding, but to more fully rely on Your grace and mercy as You order my steps and work all things out for my good.

One Minute of Praise:

What are some of the hard things you are facing now? What are the battles you have been fighting that you know you should give over to the Lord through praise? Think of one of those hard places and write down every reason that comes to mind why you can trust God for the answer.

_____

_____

_____

_____

_____

_____

_____

_____

FIFTY

The Path into His Presence

But the hour cometh, and now is, when the true worshippers shall worship the Father in spirit and in truth: for the Father seeketh such to worship him. God is a Spirit: and they that worship him must worship him in spirit and in truth.

John 4:23,24 KJV

The key purpose of praise—separately from merely glorifying the magnificent works of God—is to bring you into the presence of God so that you can worship Him in spirit and in truth.

"God is Spirit," means that God is not a physical being limited to one place. He is present everywhere, and He can be worshiped anywhere, at any time. It is not where you worship that counts, but how you worship.

Is your praise and worship genuine and true? Do you have the Holy Spirit's help? How does the Holy Spirit facilitate your praise and worship? Not only does the Holy Spirit give you greater wisdom and understanding of the Word—as well as speaking to you in those dark moments assuring you of His love—but He also prays intensely for you.

Romans 8:26,27 states,

And the Holy Spirit helps us in our distress. For we don't even know what we should pray for, nor how we should pray. But the Holy Spirit prays for us with groanings that cannot be expressed in words. And the Father who knows all hearts knows what the Spirit is saying, for the Spirit pleads for us believers in harmony with God's own will.

Romans 5:5 tells us how much He loves us.

And this expectation will not disappoint us. For we know how dearly God loves us, because he has given us the Holy Spirit to fill our hearts with his love.

With all this loving care He gives us, how can we do less than continually offer Him our unreserved praise? If you are ever in doubt, or find yourself without inspiration, here are ten reasons to praise Him every moment of everyday:

1.   Praise builds faith in times of fear.

Be not afraid nor dismayed by reason of this great multitude; for the battle is not yours, but God's.

2 Chronicles 20:15 KJV

2.   Praise releases a heart of gratitude.

How grateful I am, and how I praise the Lord!

Philippians 4:10

3.   Praise connects to God.

Come near to God and he will come near to you.

James 4:8 NIV

4.   Praise protects you from the adversary.

I will call on the Lord, who is worthy of praise, for he saves me from my enemies.

Psalm 18:3

5.   Praise satisfies your loneliness.

For he satisfies the thirsty and fills the hungry with good things.

Psalm 107:9

6.   Praise welcomes the presence of the Lord.

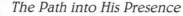

Because of Christ and our faith in him, we can now come fearlessly into God's presence, assured of his glad welcome.

Ephesians 3:12-13

7.   Praise turns your anguish into His Word.

Casting all your care upon him; for he cares for you.

1 Peter 5:7 NKJV

8.   Praise refreshes your soul.

He restoreth my soul.

Psalm 23:3 KJV

9.   Praise promotes the supernatural.

And at midnight Paul and Silas prayed, and sang praises unto God...and suddenly there was a great earthquake...immediately all the doors were opened, and everyone's bands were loosed.

Acts 16:25,26 KJV

10. Praise reminds you of the benefits you have in Christ:

Bless the Lord, O my soul, and forget not all his benefits: who forgiveth all thine iniquities; who healeth all thy diseases; who redeemeth thy life from destruction; who crowneth thee with lovingkindness

and tender mercies; who satisfieth thy mouth with good things; so that thy youth is renewed like the eagle's.

Psalm 103:2-5 KJV

Take a moment and invite the presence of Jehovah God to visit you right where you are. Speak forth words of thanksgiving, sing a song, quote a scripture, dance around the room, clap your hands, shout out with a loud voice—whatever it takes to get God's attention—do it! It will be worth it!

Lord, You are worthy to be praised! I praise You today for all Your goodness and mercy toward me, all the good things You have provided, and all the love You have bestowed on those who love You. I praise You with all my heart, mind, and strength! Help me today to make my praise more pleasing to You. Teach me to dance with You, and rejoice before You! Show me how to make my love more known to You, and Your love more known to everyone I meet.

Think over all the good reasons to praise God now. Meditate on each of the ten reasons previously listed and see if you can add a few of your own—for one minute.

Putting Praise into Action

FIFTY-ONE

Keeping a Praise Focus

Look carefully then how you walk! Live purposefully and worthily and accurately, not as the unwise and witless, but as wise (sensible, intelligent people), making the very most of the time [buying up each opportunity], because the days are evil. Therefore do not be vague and thoughtless and foolish, but understanding and firmly grasping what the will of the Lord is.

Ephesians 5:15-17 AMP

*D*o you experience distractions in your devotional time, praise time, and prayer time? You try to give Him one minute of praise, spend time in the Word or prayer, but your mind wanders and you find yourself thinking about what you are going to fix for supper, what you need to accomplish before the day is over, what someone said to you at work yesterday, who you have a meeting with tomorrow, and the list goes on. Before you know it, your mind has wandered miles away from where you started and devotion time is up. Then you begin to feel condemned.

Or you read your Bible, but you're just reading words. You begin to praise him and there is no meaning coming out of your mouth. You enter into prayer and dullness overcomes you. You think, maybe I'll just go check my e-mail and get back to prayer later. Then later never comes.

Instead of focusing on God, you feel the pressure of the demands hovering around you. Only now you feel guilty, condemned, and alienated as if you are the only person who is struggling with this problem.

You even say to yourself, "Tomorrow will be better"— but tomorrow never comes.

If you find yourself continuously battling this sort of distraction, you are not alone. The enemy of your soul is on special assignment to keep you distracted from pursuing the presence of God. This "assignment of distraction" is designed to overtake your mind and keep you in the mire the Bible calls "the cares of this world." Distractions—if not overcome—will eventually bring destruction.

Satan finds strength in distractions; because he knows your strength comes from your focus on God through your praise, prayer, and devotional time. Your strength is not in yourself, your talents or your gifts—it comes from focusing on the Lord. If your heart is full of praise, prayer, and the Word, you are going to be soaring in the days ahead. You will go from natural to supernatural—from ordinary to extraordinary. Satan's aim is to distract you from that—one trivial detail at a time.

In Luke chapter ten, Martha invites Jesus into her home, but she becomes so distracted with entertaining that she neglects being present and enjoying His company. Jesus did not condemn Martha for her work, but he drew her attention to her distractedness.

Life is full of distractions. If it is difficult for you to find time to spend with the Lord, you may need to reset your priorities. Many times it's as simple as making a list. Begin by putting the most important thing that you need to accomplish for the day at the top. Lists for the next day are great to make right before you go to bed. You may say, "I don't like to make lists," or "It takes too much time. I just want to go to bed and go to sleep," believe me, you will save at least an hour the next day by prioritizing your schedule the night before—an hour you can use to get quiet before God.

For myself, I prioritize my time on a daily basis, then weekly, and then monthly. I make a list of the most important things I should focus on each day, each week, and then each month. I get much more accomplished by knowing where I am going and knowing my time frame. After I make my list, I go back over it and cross off what someone else can do, or what can wait. At the very top of every list, I put the time I will set aside for the Lord. If I don't allocate a specific time for Him, schedule an appointment with Him, the day will pass and I'll have accomplished everything but spending time with the Lord. Then, not only have I missed out on the most powerful, turbo-charged opportunity I have available to me each day, but I'm rendered even more powerless by the resulting condemnation.

Don't let the enemy have his way with you and your destiny. Redeem the time, make the most of every opportunity, be vigilant, and be diligent with the precious few hours you have been given each day. Be a good steward. For God to use you as a vessel of honor, you must be circumspect and ruthless with your time. That doesn't mean "doing more" – that means "being more." Becoming "a vessel of honor prepared for every good work" (2 Timothy 2:21) involves the work of being, not the work of doing. The work of being, or becoming, is done at the feet of Jesus—by spending time in His presence. When you invest yourself—your time—in being with Him, He can then release you into the right doing.

When you spend time "abiding in Him"—abiding in grace—everything becomes clear and uncomplicated. In His presence you become complete. When He is in you there are no mountains too big or devils too mean that can distract you. When you've spent time with the Lord, once you open your mouth and speak forth the Word, every weapon formed against you will be disarmed and powerless.

Make time for God. In His presence you will find fullness of joy, and that joy is your strength. Don't get distracted from the mother lode of heaven by chasing fool's gold here on earth. Put God on the throne of your heart by making Him ruler of your time—one minute at a time.

Lord, You are my priority! Holy Spirit, help me each day to keep my priorities straight and not to get stuck in the mire of distractions. Help me to guard my heart and mind with Your peace, Lord—to be still and know You are God. I will seek You first before anything else. My soul longs after You!

One Minute of Praise:

Of all the things on your plate to do, which can keep you from the love of God? Position your heart to seek Him first by giving Him glory in this moment now—for one whole minute.

FIFTY-TWO

Building a Strong Tower

Glory and honour are in his presence; strength and gladness are in his place.

1 Chronicles 16:27 KJV

Thou wilt shew me the path of life: in thy presence is fullness of joy; at thy right hand there are pleasures for evermore.

Psalm 16:11 KJV

In Him you find strength, gladness, joy, your path of life, and pleasure forever. All this is yours when you invite

Him to spend a day with you. How do you invite Him to spend all day with you? The invitation comes through you preparing a place for Him to reign.

Just as Esther prepared herself to enter the court where King Xerxes was sitting on his throne, your praise opens a pathway for the King of Kings to sit upon his throne right where you are. Psalm 22:3 HCSB declares, "But You are holy, enthroned on the praises of Israel." Your praise creates a throne for Him to rule in your situation.

Why is a throne so important? The throne is where the king gives out instructions, orders, and edicts. The words released from the king's throne must be carried out. There is no higher place of authority in any kingdom than the throne from where the king issues his decrees and judgements. All orders are given and carried out from the throne.

Your praise builds a throne in your life from where God can rule. Your praise clears out a territorial position in the atmosphere around you from where Christ's authority in you must be heeded. Your praises testifying to God's faithfulness don't return to earth void, but must accomplish all God has set forth His Word to do. God is King and His Word is law, but you must enthrone the King through your praises for His Word to reign in your life.

Build a throne of grace in your home, at your workplace, on the streets. Bring His presence with you wherever you go by continually offering Him praises and giving thanks. Let the grace of God reign in your household, on the job, and in your community. You will find the lost getting saved, your financial pressures being erased, your job becoming pleasant, and the course of governments being redirected. Pray for the Prince of Peace to rule in your heart, your family, and even on the other side of the world. The grace of God comes to dwell by invitation only.

Your unsaved friends and family will get uncomfortable when they are around you, but at the same time they will be attracted to the peace that is inside of you. When someone at work needs prayer, who do they go to? They will come to you because they know you are connected.

Meanwhile, the spirit of the world trembles because the Jesus inside of you is your hope of glory. Demonic spirits can't hang around to torment your mind, sidetrack you, or set up distractions because the power inside of you rules over all.

Isaiah 59:19 KJV says,

So shall they fear the name of the Lord from the west, and his glory from the rising of the sun. When the enemy shall come in like a flood, the Spirit of the Lord shall lift up a standard against him.

That standard is you! God in you shows up and sets the captives free!

Building a Strong Tower

I like to move the comma after the word "flood" in that verse and place it after the word "in." In that case it would read like this, "When the enemy shall come in, like a flood the Spirit of the Lord shall lift up a standard against him." *The Spirit of God in you will flood the enemy.*

God is looking for a group of men and women who know their God, not just know a program, not just know how to stay busy, but know their God for Who He is, What He is, and Where He is.

He is looking for a people whose heart is completely His. Like David said, "My heart is fixed on Him." (See Isaiah 26:3.) Your heart must be prepared for duty—a heart fixed on God without distractions—a heart prepared to do His will, not your own.

The Lord is looking for a righteousness remnant. A remnant that will stand up and say, "I choose this day whom I will serve. I choose this day to praise my God, the Holy One of Israel. I choose this day for the King of Kings to sit upon the throne that I have formed with my praise."

It does not matter where you live, how much money you have, what color your skin is, where you work, or if you lost your job yesterday. Your mission today, if you choose to accept it, is to create a throne for Him to sit upon to rule over your enemy and watch over your day. He is enthroned on the praises of His people—and that's you!

Lord, reveal the schemes and tricks of the enemy, and help me speak words that will stop the enemy from advancing. Forgive me for not praising You in the face of my enemies, for not speaking words of faith during times of crisis, and most of all, for not putting You first. Holy Spirit, wake me early and compel me each morning to let praise be the first words spoken from my lips. Help me to consecrate my evening, turn in early, and praise You with my last breath before I sleep. Lord, keep my heart fixed on You.

One Minute of Praise:

Fix your heart on the Lord. Be still and know that He is God—for the next minute.

Building a Strong Tower

FIFTY-THREE

Making the Sacrifice

Therefore I will offer sacrifices of joy in His tabernacle; I will sing, yes, I will sing praises to the Lord.

Psalm 27:6 NKJV

With Jesus' help, let us continually offer our sacrifice of praise to God by proclaiming the glory of his name.

Hebrews 13:15

There is only one thing that can stop you from giving a sacrifice of praise and that is if you have nothing to offer God. But who has nothing at all to offer God? In Leviticus 27:9 KJV we read, "And if it be a beast, whereof men bring an offering unto the Lord, all that any man giveth unto the

Lord shall be holy." Look at 1 Chronicles 16:29 KJV: "Give unto the Lord the glory due unto his name: bring an offering, and come before him: worship the Lord in the beauty of holiness." And then Psalm 96:8,9 KJV tells us, "Give unto the Lord the glory due unto his name: bring an offering, and come into his courts." In these scripture you see a sacrifice of praise is a commandment that—if obeyed— becomes holy and pleasing to God.

You may say, "But I don't have anything to give. I don't have a job. My husband has left me and he was my source of income. I filed bankruptcy this year. I'm sick and can't even leave my house." Let me ask you this, "What do you think you posses that your Heavenly Father wants the most besides your praise?" You may be surprised to know, God doesn't want your stuff, your money, your talents, or your gifts. Even though all those are important to give to Him so He can release blessings in your life, the real answer is: He wants YOU. When you truly give yourself to him, everything you possess becomes His and His responsibility to take care of. Your stuff, your money, your talents, your gifts, your job, your family—it all comes with the package of YOU. The end result? You and everything about you becomes holy. What is Holy? Well, for starters, holy means "blessed!" Do you desire to be blessed? I know I do!

David was the most unlikely person that anyone would have chosen to be king over Israel, but God saw something in him that no one else did. God saw his heart. God saw

Making the Sacrifice

that David was faithful and obedient to do and give what God asked. David's sacrifice of praise was himself. He laid himself upon the altar and said, "I give it all, Lord. Take me and use me. I might be the runt in the family and not that good looking, but I will be faithful with what you have given me." Whether it was his shepherd's staff taking care of the sheep or a sword bringing down Goliath, David laid himself upon the altar as his sacrifice of praise. I'm sure David made many altars as he took care of the sheep and sang praises to the Lord day after day and night after night. The end result was he became the apple of God's eye!

Noah was another man who made a sacrifice of praise. In Genesis 8:20 it says that "after the flood, Noah built an altar to the Lord and taking some of all the clean animals he sacrificed burnt offerings." You know he was praising God after he and his family survived the flood and found dry land! But it must have been bittersweet. Noah saw such incredible destruction. Think about it. All of mankind drowned around him—and although he and his family were saved—he had to shut his ears to the wailing of all humanity perishing. It's hard to fathom the anguish that Noah would have had to endure, and yet he was still obedient to God's instruction.[5]

How powerful was his sacrifice of praise? Genesis 8:21 KJV tells us,

And the Lord smelled a sweet savour; and the Lord said in his heart, I will not again curse the ground any more for man's sake; for the imagination of man's heart is evil from his youth; neither will I again smite any more every thing living, as I have done.

God promised He would never again curse the ground because of man, even though God knew that by nature man would always be unthankful. Why do you think God gave us that covenant promise? Because there was one man by the name of Noah who gave God praise even while living through extremely unpleasant circumstances—he didn't neglect to praise God in the midst of it all. His sacrifice of praise reached heaven and was pleasing to God.

We find yet another story in Genesis 26 about Isaac becoming a very wealthy and prosperous man. As his crops, his flocks of sheep and goats, and his herds of cattle continued to grow, the Philistines became jealous of him. They closed up all of Isaac's wells with dirt. These were the wells dug by the servants of his father, Abraham. Then Abimelech asked him to leave the country. "'Go somewhere else,' he said, 'for you have become too rich and powerful for us'" (Genesis 26:16).

Everywhere Isaac moved, he dug wells, the springs would gush forth with water, he would flourish, and the people would become jealous and fearful and ask him to leave again and again. On the night of their arrival in Beer-sheba, the Lord appeared to him saying,

I am the God of your father, Abraham. Do not be afraid for I am with you and will bless you. I will give you many descendants, and they will become a great nation. I will do this because of my promise to Abraham, my servant.

Genesis 26:24

Isaac then built an altar and offered the Lord his sacrifice of praise. God had poured His blessings upon Isaac and Isaac knew from where they had come. He did not neglect to give glory where glory was due.

It would have been very easy for Isaac to become discouraged after the first move, but after three moves he remained praiseful. Isaac knew that God was his source, not man. God had promised, "I am with you, do not be afraid." Isaac knew he had to take time to give the God of his universe a praise offering.

Another sacrifice of praise was when Abraham built an altar, bound up his son, and offered Isaac to the Lord. He reached out his hand, took up his knife to slay the most precious gift that God had given him, and suddenly an angel appeared and stopped him. The Lord saw that he was willing to give the thing closest to his heart as a sacrifice.

One Minute of Praise

Abraham was willing to give whatever sacrifice God asked of him. All God asks of you is to give Him a sacrifice of praise.

Father God, I give You praise and glory! I give You my heart, my mind, and my body as a living sacrifice. I bring You my worship and words of love, and lay them at the foot of Your Throne. May my worship be pleasing to You, and my praises a sweet smelling fragrance. Teach me to love You as David did. Teach me to bring You glory as I bless Your Holy Name!

One Minute of Praise:

Build an altar in your heart now and make your sacrifice—for one minute.

FIFTY-FOUR

Praise That Changes History

David built there an altar to the Lord and offered burnt offerings and peace offerings. So the Lord heeded the prayers for the land, and Israel's plague was stayed.

II Samuel 24:25 AMP

*J*n 2 Kings 20, we read about a king by the name of Hezekiah and the prophet Isaiah. King Hezekiah had become deathly ill and sent for Isaiah. Isaiah told the king that he would not recover from this illness and that he would surely die. That was not the news the king wanted to hear. The king turned his face toward the wall as Isaiah was leaving and prayed to the Lord. He reminded the Lord how faithful he had been and how he had done what was pleasing in His sight. He reminded the Lord how his father had locked the doors of the temple so the people were unable to place their offerings upon the altar. He reminded the Lord that when he became king he reopened the temple so the people could once again offer their sacrifices to God. He then broke down and wept bitterly.

Before Isaiah could leave the courtyard, a message came to him from the Lord. The Lord told Isaiah, "Go back to Hezekiah, the leader of my people. Tell him, 'This is what the Lord, the God of your ancestor David, says: I have heard your prayer and seen your tears, I will heal you, and three days from now you will get out of bed and go to the Temple of the Lord. I will add fifteen years to your life, and I will rescue you and this city from the king of Assyria. I will do this to defend My honor and for the sake of My servant, David,'" Isaiah did just that and Hezekiah recovered.

What is significant in this story? When God was reminded of the reopening of the Temple and its altars, God seemed to have a change of heart. He not only healed Hezekiah within three days, but added fifteen years to his life. A sacrifice placed upon the altar of God was so significant that it changed history for King Hezekiah.

Another example of history changing praise is found in II Samuel 24. We read in this chapter that David had become a very prideful and ambitious man. He was seeking glory and power. By doing this he put his faith in the size of his army rather than in God's protection. So the Lord sent a prophet by the name of Gad to tell David, "This is what the Lord says: I will give you three choices. Choose one of these punishments, and I will do it" (v. 11). God was punishing David for his pride. God gave him three choices: 1) three years of famine, 2) three months of fleeing from the enemy, or 3) three days of severe plague. It's a little hard to comprehend God allowing you to choose your own punishment for sinning, but God knew what he was doing.

In verse seventeen David tells the Lord, "I am the one who has sinned and done wrong! But these people are innocent—what have they done? Let Your anger fall against me and my family." Perhaps God wanted David to come clean and admit that he was in error. It was he, after all, not the people, who had the gloating attitude. However, many times our sins have repercussions on the people around us. It seems unfair that our family and friends should reap what we sow, but this is an example of that very thing.

David chose the shortest punishment for the sake of his people: three days of plague. That same day Gad went to David and told him to go and build an altar to the Lord on the threshing floor of Araunah the Jebusite. David negotiated a price and purchased the threshing floor, built an altar unto the Lord, and offered burnt offerings and peace offerings. The story concludes by telling us, "And the Lord answered his prayer, and the plague was stopped."

Aren't you glad that God hears your prayers when you pray? They are never put on hold or lost in delivery. God hears and answers prayer. Our repentance with our sacrifice of praise can immediately prevent the people we love from getting hurt for our sake.

Thank you Lord for Your endless grace and abundant mercy! Praise You for Your goodness, kindness, and compassion. Holy Father, thank you for not giving us what we deserve, or withholding from us the blessings we don't deserve. Praise You for gently teaching us and leading us into the way of truth.

One Minute of Praise:

Can you think of a time when God didn't give you what you deserved, or gave you something wonderful you didn't deserve? Praise and thank Him for it now.

_____

_____

_____

_____

Praise That Changes History

FIFTY-FIVE

How to Build an Altar of Praise

Therefore, the angel of the Lord commanded Gad to say to David that David should go and erect an altar to the Lord on the threshing floor of Ornan the Jebusite.

1 Chronicles 21:18 NKJV

What is so significant about an altar? *Altar* is defined as "a high place of praise and worship on which sacrifices are offered or incense is burned." (See Merriam-Webster Online.) There are four elements that you need to create an altar upon which to offer your sacrifices of praise.

First, you need a place to build your altar. Where do you build an altar? You may think you have to load your car down with stones, mix cement, and find a piece of land to build an altar, but I have good news for you. After God sent His Son to this earth as His sacrifice, your altar is anywhere you are. It could be at home, in your car, at work, in the back yard, pushing your cart down the grocery aisle, or sitting in a hospital waiting room. It's your private place, your inner sanctuary, wherever you are whether sitting, standing, or lying down.

Secondly, you need praise. Where does praise come from? In Hebrews 13:15 KJV, Paul tells us, "Let us offer the sacrifice of praise to God continually, that is, the fruit of our lips giving thanks to his name." All you need to do is open your mouth and begin bragging on God. The more you brag on God the higher your praise goes. Before long your praise begins to invade heaven. You will find yourself in a secret place with Him that no one can enter by force. The distraction of kids, cars, barking dogs, and noisy neighbors become muted. It's just you and Him.

Thirdly, you need a sacrifice. That's easy. It's you. This time it's all about you—the things that are consuming you— your selfish desires. Whatever is pulling you away from God—such as the demands of the world, cares, concerns, whatever weighs on your heart—steals your joy or chastises your peace. Instead of letting these things be distractions, put them all on the altar before God and watch them all go up in smoke.

Lastly, you place yourself upon the altar and say, "Lord I give you my all today. Let your praise fill this earthly temple all day long; when I feel like it and when I don't feel like it." As your sacrifice of praise goes up, the Lord sends the fire of the Holy Spirit to consume you with peace, comfort, strength, wisdom, knowledge, and power. Your flesh man will turn to ashes as your spirit man rises up with power and authority. You won't be able to stop praising Him! It will go on all day long—a minute here, and a minute there. It becomes contagious. Your family and co-workers take notice of a different you. And it all began on the altar.

The Word says David built his altar upon a threshing floor. What is so significant about a threshing floor? The altar is a place of high praise but the threshing floor is a place of separation. As I have previously mentioned, the threshing floor was a place where freshly harvested wheat was placed to be trampled by oxen and "threshed" to separate the wheat from the chaff. The grain had to go through a threshing process to remove the dry covering from the seeds. As long as the wheat was on the threshing floor, it was guarded by family members to protect it from thieves. It is on the threshing floor where the Lord breaks and molds us into His likeness. And He will not leave us unguarded while that is happening.

The altar, on the other hand, represents a high place where you brag on God's character. You begin to thank Him for Who He is:

Jehovah-Jireh: Lord, You are my Provider.

Jehovah-Raphah: The Lord my Healer.

Jehovah-Nissi: The Lord my Banner.

Jehovah-Shalom: The Lord my Peace.

Jehovah-Ra-ah: The Lord my Shepard.

Jehovah-Tsidkenu: He is the Lord my Righteousness.

Jehovah-Shammah: The Lord is always present.

When these two elements—the altar and the threshing floor—come together, you see that not only sacrificial praise, but also repentance and forgiveness, all the stuff that has hindered your praise has not only been *separated* from you—but completely forgotten.

Help me, Holy Spirit, to meet You on the threshing floor of my heart. Help me to separate myself and to meet You on the high places. Purify my heart, my thoughts, my words—make me a vessel of Your honor—a vessel of purest gold that pours out the sweetest oil of praise, joy, and thanksgiving.

One Minute of Praise:

What do you have to place as a sacrifice on your altar? Do it right now—for one minute.

_____

_____

_____

_____

_____

_____

_____

XII.

Praises New Every Morning

FIFTY-SIX

Restoring Passionate Praise

Then he turned toward the woman and said to Simon, "Do you see this woman? I came into your house. You did not give me any water for my feet, but she wet my feet with her tears and wiped them with her hair. You did not give me a kiss, but this woman, from the time I entered, has not stopped kissing my feet. You did not put oil on my head, but she has poured perfume on my feet. Therefore, I tell you, her many sins have been forgiven—for she loved much."

Luke 7:44-47 NIV

*T*he woman in this story, mentioned in chapter eighteen, did something the others knew to do, but for some unknown reason, didn't. Every person understood that common courtesy required the feet of honored guests to be washed—but by now, Jesus was just one of the boys. As time passed, He became a Celestial Chum. A chumming relationship is the forerunner to a casual relationship. The more casual we become in the presence of God, the more superficial we become with our praise.[6]

The Lord became just another one of the guys. After all, they saw Him get ticked off when God's House was converted into a flea market. They saw Him spit on the ground, make a mud ball, and rub it over a man's blind eye. They saw Him indebted to the state and in need of a financial miracle so that a fish had to vomit up money to pay His taxes. He even enjoyed going to parties like they did, and turned water into wine when the host ran out. They watched as he fell asleep in the back of a boat, snoring through a storm. They saw him eat with tax collectors and notorious sinners—even the Pharisees questioned why he ate with such scum. They saw Him hungry, tired, and cranky.

Their constant exposure to His humanity blinded their vision of His priceless, precious Divinity. They saw the Savior when He was weary and sunburned. They saw the Master with mud under His fingernails and dirt between His toes. This guy they wandered around with was basically a homeless carpenter's son. To them, the King of the universe was just another one of the boys who had dropped by for a glass of wine and a chat about the economy.

Can you imagine what they must have thought when this uninvited, repulsive woman showed up out of nowhere? She was a party crasher! But this particular woman crashed the party for one reason and one reason only. She wanted to be in the presence of God Himself. Although being that close to Christ the Lord must have made her nervous, she would not be intimidated by the others' condescending looks or comments. With a pounding heart, she reached for one of His feet and began to wash it with her tears. She did with love what others should have done out of courtesy and respect.

The tears from her cheeks splashed on His feet. They were mingled with the sweat and dirt. It was not her place to wash His feet, but His teachings had given her a new direction in life and her heart demanded a bold gesture of gratitude. Perhaps she had accepted Him as her Lord during one of His crusades as He talked about sins being forgiven. She had infinite adoration for the One who had shown her matchless grace. Her passion for His presence made it her pleasure to give Him this extravagant praise.[7]

Time tarnishes treasures. I have several pieces of silver in my dining room. If I do not take proper care of them, over time they will begin to tarnish. What was once a precious gift to me then becomes dull and loses its luster and value.

It is not any different with our attitudes toward our Heavenly Father. We must treat Him with the respect He deserves and give Him the honor due His Name. If we only come to Him when we need Him, our reverence and "fear of the Lord" will sit on a shelf and tarnish, losing the luster of His Presence in our life. He is God. If it were not for Him, we would not have breath to breathe nor the strength to get out of bed. He deserves more than an occasional phone call from us!

When passion is missing, important things become unimportant, and necessary things become unnecessary. When we have extravagant passion, reading the Word, talking to our Heavenly Father, paying our tithes, attending church, filling our mouth with continual praise, and loving one another in the Body of Christ are basic necessities that bring joy; but when passion fades, these necessary components become less and less important and our existence more and more dull.

Praise is the result of passion. Extravagant passion gripped the heart of Simon Peter, James, John, Andrew, and Philip to walk away from prosperous fishing businesses and follow a Man with no permanent home and no full-time job. They would follow Him all day long to no-name cities just to go about doing good, guessing where they would be sleeping, and wondering what they would be doing the next day. Passion tugged at the heart of Matthew and pulled him away from a prosperous career as a tax collector. Passion overcame Bartholomew, Thomas, James, Thaddaeus, and Judas to leave everything and follow a Man they knew very little about. He did not promise them riches or honor, title or position—but a passion possessed each of them to simply be in His presence.

It took a sinner woman, an alabaster box, and two tired, dirty feet to revive the love and passion of Christ's disciples.

Forgive us, Lord, when our hearts grow cold. Stir within us a passion for Your presence—a consuming thirst and yearning to be closer to You. Teach us to not only sit at Your feet, but to wash them and anoint them with a sweet smelling perfume of our praise.

One Minute of Praise:

Break the alabaster box of your heart on the feet of Jesus right now—for one minute.

FIFTY-SEVEN

In a Blaze of Praise

*Rejoice ye in that day, and leap for joy: for, behold,
your reward is great in heaven.*

Luke 6:23 KJV

The Lord's disciples lived and died in a blaze of praise!
To die such extravagant deaths for their Lord and Savior could only have been made possible by living a lifestyle
of extreme praise. Look at how those who loved their Lord
went home to heaven:

- Stephen was stoned to death.

- James had his head chopped off.

- Simon Peter was crucified upside down.

- James at ninety-four, was beaten, stoned, and finally clubbed to death.

- John was dropped into a pot of boiling oil up to his armpits.

- Andrew was crucified on a cross upside down.

- Philip was scourged, thrown into prison, and afterwards crucified.

- Bartholomew was cruelly beaten and then crucified.

- Matthew was slain by an ax blade.

- Thomas had a spear thrust through his upper body.

- Simon the Zealot was crucified.

- Thaddaeus was crucified.

- Mark was dragged down the city streets to his death.

- Matthias was first stoned then decapitated.

- Luke was hung on an olive tree.

- Paul was decapitated.

Imagine walking with Jesus in person day after day, listening to Him teach the Beatitudes—seeing people being raised from the dead, eyes given sight, deaf ears opened, the lame leaping with joy. The adventure of walking with Jesus was worth the price of dying for His cause. Their reward after death was even greater than the privilege of walking with Him in the flesh.

A story is told about the execution of Polycarp, one of the Apostle John's disciples. John pastored in Smyrna. When Polycarp was being burned at the stake for refusing to deny Christ, he said: "Wherefore also I praise Thee for all things, I bless Thee, I glorify Thee, along with the everlasting and heavenly Jesus Christ, Thy beloved Son, with Whom, to Thee and the Holy Ghost be glory both now and to all coming ages."

When the fire was kindled around his body and began to blaze up and overtake him, eyewitnesses said, "He appeared as gold or silver, glowing in a furnace. We began to smell a sweet odor coming from the pile, as if frankincense or such precious spices was being burned," just like in the Tabernacle when the high priest would pour incense over the coals in the incense burner and a sweet-smelling smoke would fill the room of the inner court. The burning incense would press against the veil being drawn by the Presence of God that was behind it. As Polycarp was placed upon his incense burner, praise began to pour from within him—inhaled as a sweet-smelling odor in the nostrils of God. I can hear the Lord saying, "Well done, good and faithful servant; thou hast been faithful over a few things, I will make thee ruler over many things: enter thou into the joy of thy Lord" (Matthew 25:23).

The men who watched could not believe that this "strange man" would not burn. They finally commanded an executioner to pierce a dagger through his heart. When he

In a Blaze of Praise

did this, to their surprise, a dove flew out of his chest with such a great quantity of blood that the fire was extinguished.

What will it take to revive, rejuvenate, restore, reawaken, regenerate, and rekindle your love for Him? When will you become as passionate as that for the pleasure of His Presence?

Your praise will cost you something. It might be your time, perhaps a sacrifice of your attitude, or putting the tongue to death. You cannot allow the presence of your problem to keep you from pursuing the Presence of your King. Oh, the reward is so much greater than the cost! What could be more magnificent than resting in His Presence, not just once, but everyday for the rest of your life? Yes, it is possible for His presence to encompass you twenty-four hours a day, seven days a week. The window of His presence is opened through your praise. It's time to take a break for one minute of praise!

Father God, help me to love You extravagantly everyday, with every breath, and every word. Holy Spirit, teach me how to live a lifestyle so ablaze with praise, that not one day is wasted by neglecting to offer You my extreme praise! You are the Lord of Lords, the King of Kings, majestic and awesome— You are the power and the glory forever! I worship You with all I am, while I am—and like the disciples before me, may I leave this place in a blaze of praise!

One Minute of Praise:

If you can't praise the Lord extravagantly when life is going "as usual," how can you expect to go through your "day of reckoning" in a blaze of praise? Start practicing right now living ablaze so you'll be prepared to leave in a blaze—for one minute.

FIFTY-EIGHT

Laus Deo!

You are awesome, O God, in your sanctuary; the God of Israel gives power and strength to his people.

Psalm 68:35 NIV

*O*n the aluminum cap atop the Washington Monument in Washington, DC, are displayed two words: *Laus Deo*. Standing in front of this monument you are unable to see these words—in fact, most visitors to the monument are totally unaware they are even there—but these words have been there for years. They are 555 feet by 5.125 inches high. Perched atop the monument, they face skyward to the Father of our Nation, overlooking the 69 square miles which comprise the District of Columbia and the capital of the United States of America.

One Minute of Praise

Laus Deo! Two seemingly insignificant, and certainly unnoticed, words—inscribed in a place that no passerby can read them. You might think since they are so out of sight that they would be equally out of mind, but not so! They are positioned in a very meaningful place at the highest point over what is the most powerful city of the most successful nation in the world! And they have remained inscribed on the minds of Americans all across the nation for all these generations.

But what do these two small, Latin words mean? Very simply, "Praise be to God!" Although construction of this giant obelisk began in 1848 when James Polk was President of the United States, it was not until 1888 that the monument was inaugurated and opened to the public. It took twenty-five years to finally cap the memorial with a tribute to the true Father of our Nation: *Laus Deo* – "Praise be to God!"

From atop this magnificent granite and marble structure, visitors may take in the beautiful panoramic view of the city with its four major divisions. From that vantage point, one can also easily see the original plan of the designer, Pierre Charles l'Enfant: a perfect cross with the White House to the north, the Jefferson Memorial to the south, the Capital to the east, and the Lincoln Memorial to the west.

A cross you might ask? Why a cross? What about separation of church and state? Yes, the layout of the central governing district of our nation is in the shape of a cross.

Laus Deo!

Separation of church and state was not, and is not, in the Constitution. This was no doubt intended to carry a profound meaning for those who bothered to notice. *Praise be to God!*

Within the monument itself are 898 steps and 50 landings. As one climbs the steps and pauses on the landings, the memorial stones share a very specific message. On the 12th landing is a prayer offered by the City of Baltimore; on the 20th is a memorial presented by a group of Chinese Christians; on the 24th is a presentation made by Sunday School children from New York and Philadelphia including the following scripture quotations:

The memory of the righteous is blessed: But the name of the wicked will rot.

Proverbs 10:7 NKJV

Train up a child in the way he should go: and when he is old, he will not depart from it.

Proverbs 22:6 KJV

But Jesus called them unto them, and said, "Suffer little children to come unto me, and forbid them not: for of such is the kingdom of God."

Luke 18:16 KJV

In addition to these biblical messages, the cornerstone of the Washington Monument, which was laid on July 4th,

1848, holds a Holy Bible presented to Congress by the Bible Society as a symbol of God's Word being a cornerstone of our government. Such was the discipline, the moral direction, and the spiritual mood given by the founder and first President of our unique democracy that is still summed up on every piece of American currency: "In God We Trust."

I was awed by the prayer spoken by President Washington:

Almighty God; we make our earnest prayer that Thou wilt keep the United States in Thy holy protection; that Thou wilt incline the hearts of the citizens to cultivate a spirit of subordination and obedience to government; and entertain a brotherly affection and love for one another and for their fellow citizens of the United States at large. And finally that Thou wilt most graciously be pleased to dispose us all to do justice, to love mercy, and to demean ourselves with charity, humility, and pacific temper of mind which were the characteristics of the Divine Author of our blessed religion, and without a humble imitation of whose example in these things we can never hope to be a happy nation. Grant our supplication, we beseech Thee, through Jesus Christ our Lord. Amen.

You may forget the width and height of the words, "*Laus Deo,*" their location, or the architects who masterminded the

 Laus Deo!   275

Washington Monument, but no one who reads this will be able to forget their meaning—"Praise be to God"—or the verse found in Psalm 127:1 NIV, "Unless the Lord builds the house, its builders labor in vain. Unless the Lord watches over the city, the watchmen stand guard in vain."

Lord, help us to remember our heritage as Americans. Let us not forget the foundation upon which our nation was built. Remind us daily that "In God we trust" and that we are indeed "one nation under God"— for our only hope for peace and prosperity is in You. May we continue to seek Your face and Your blessing as we boldly pray to You, Father God, in Jesus' name, to stand beside our nation, and guide her.

One Minute of Praise:

Take a minute to praise God for this nation.

FIFTY-NINE

Don't Let the Rocks Replace Your Praise

I tell you that, if these should hold their peace, the stones would immediately cry out.

Luke 19:40 KJV

This past summer my husband Randel and I visited Ground Zero in New York and the White House in Washington, DC. As I stood in total silence to observe the inscriptions that surrounded Ground Zero and other public places all over our nation's capitol, I easily found the signature of God, as it is unmistakably inscribed everywhere we looked. The words, "God Bless America" were emblazoned everywhere—someone had even spray painted those words on the sides of buildings and overpasses.

On the morning of 9/11, we sat speechlessly watching our television along with millions of other Americans. With hands held to our hearts we muttered, "Jesus help us," "Oh Lord God," "Father in heaven, help these people." Our hearts began to pound with fear as blood rushed to our heads and we wondered, "What is happening to America?" We had to find a seat and sit down. We could not believe what was happening in the "Land of the Blessed and the Free." We used to believe things like this only happens in other countries, not America—but not anymore

As I watched during the days following this devastating event, I saw something happen across America. People didn't care about their differences anymore. People came together as one, helping each other, caring for one another, reaching out to the hurting. I watched on TV time after time as people stood on the steps of the Capitol and other public places across America singing, "God Bless America." Flags by the thousands were sold and placed in yards, in store windows, and hooked onto car windows. I had two flags myself waving in the air as I drove down the street. I was proud to be an American. I began to understand more than ever the meaning of the words, "United we stand, divided we fall." "Unity" became a major theme in churches wherever we were traveling. I now was seeing that very unity grow across our country.

One Minute of Praise

One morning as I was watching the news, the cameraman began to show the many American flags being displayed, bumper stickers on cars saying, "God Bless America," and then concluded with a video montage of a group of employees on the steps of their workplace singing "God Bless America." The Lord spoke to my heart just then and urged me to look up the word "bless." I thought to myself, "Why do I need to look up the word bless? I know what that word means. This one syllable word is all through the Bible. We pray for God to bless our children, our homes, our businesses, our finances, and our health. It means to prosper, to have more, be successful, and have the favor of God." But the Lord kept tugging at my heart to go look it up in the dictionary. I have learned from past experiences to obey the Lord when He speaks to me, so I knew God was trying to tell me something. As I turned the pages of the dictionary to the "b's," then the "bl's," my eyes finally found the word "bless"— and I was shocked and amused by what I found.

The first definition following the word bless was "to make holy." Wow! The God that watched as Americans allowed prayer to be removed from their schools, listened to arguments over the word "God" being in the Pledge of Allegiance, observed debates over separation of church and state was now being glorified by people that had no idea what they were saying! They thought they were singing "God Bless America," but in reality they are singing, "God Make America Holy." They thought they were singing about being "blessed" when they were actually calling for "holiness." That humbled me. I thought, "God you are so clever. The laws of the country and bylaws of the constitution might be interpreted that You can be removed from society, but no man has control over the Creator of this Universe. You will find a place in the heart of every American! If it means being perched atop a monument, Your name being sung in a Patriotic song, or having a group of Sunday School children give a presentation quoting Proverbs on the 24th Landing of the Washington Monument, You will get Your praise!"

The sad part of this story, though, is as time has passed, routines have returned to normal, and the flags have disappeared, the bumper stickers have begun to peel, and the fear has begun to fade. Speaking the name Jehovah God has again been replaced by stock market quotes, the latest joke, morning newspaper headlines, and weather updates on category five hurricanes moving through the Gulf of Mexico. God's heart must have been broken to see a country that He had so blessed once again turn their backs on Him as they feel He is no longer needed.

At the same time, God has His ears inclined to those who continually choose to give Him the glory and honor that He deserves. He still seeks after those who don't let circumstances remove praise from their lips—those who choose to praise Him in the good times and praise Him in the bad times. He turns to the angel Gabriel and says, "Now those are the people that I command the angels to be in charge over. They choose to praise Me when there is plenty of money in the bank, but they also choose to praise Me when they are standing in the unemployment line. They choose to praise Me for the birth of their new baby and they still choose to praise Me standing over the coffin of their tiny infant. Their praise comes from an ongoing relationship with Me, not a one-time, desperate cry for help."

In Luke 19, Jesus responded to the Pharisees after they asked Him to rebuke the disciples who began to rejoice and praise Him with a loud voice for all the mighty works they had seen. The disciples shouted, "Blessed be the king that cometh in the name of the Lord: peace in heaven, and glory in the highest!" And the Lord replied to the Pharisees, "I tell you that, if these should hold their peace, the stones would immediately cry out." (See Luke 19:37-40.)

If America refuses to rejoice and praise God for the mighty works He has done for them, words etched in the stone across America just like the words inscribed across the top of the Washington Monument will cry out and give the CEO of the universe praise instead.

Lord I pray today, please don't let the rocks replace my praise! I choose from this day forward to praise You not because I have to, but because I can. Blessed be the Name of the Lord! The Lord reigns in all the earth! Glory to the King forever!

One Minute of Praise:

This is the day that the Lord has made, rejoice and be glad—for one minute! Don't let the rocks cry out louder than you!

SIXTY

A Book of Remembrance

That night the king could not sleep; so he ordered the book of the chronicles, the record of his reign, to be brought in and read to him. It was found recorded there that Mordecai had exposed Bigthana and Teresh, two of the king's officers who guarded the doorway, who had conspired to assassinate King Xerxes. "What honor and recognition has Mordecai received for this?" the king asked. "Nothing has been done for him," his attendants answered.

Esther 6:1-3 NIV

A Book of Remembrance   283

You may not be where you're going to be, but you're sure not where you use to be! I once again quote, "forward-focused and not past-possessed." In other words, you cannot move forward by constantly looking in the review mirror. You will become an accident just waiting to happen. There is a wrong time to reflect upon the past and there is a right time to reflect upon the past. You need to be reminded from where God has brought you, but don't relive the past by saying things like, "What if I would have married Bubba instead of Melvin?" or "If I would have done this instead of that, perhaps things would be different." You cannot change your past, but you can change your future. The time to reflect back on your past is the time to thank God for what He brought you through when you thought there was no way out, when your back was against the wall and you wanted to give up. You wondered if joy would ever return and here you are now, walking in the full light of the favor of God.

There isn't anything that builds your faith more than getting out your journal and reflecting back on a time that God brought you through. When you think your praise has run out, go back a year or two and begin to read how you came home that cold wintry night and you knew if God did not provide, your utilities would be turned off within the next two days. You sat down and wrote in your journal that night, "God, all I have is You to depend upon. I don't have enough money to pay my utility bill and it's so cold outside. God, what am I going to do? God, You have never failed

One Minute of Praise

me, and so I'm leaning on You, Heavenly Father. Lord, I got the final notice in the mail today that if this bill is not paid within forty-eight hours I will have no heat. God if you could put coins in a fish's mouth to pay taxes, you can provide the money for my heat." You close your journal and with tears coursing down your face you head to bed The next day at work, a co-worker comes up and says, "This may sound a little strange, but last night right before I went to bed, the Lord spoke to me and told me I needed to give you this $100 bill. I don't know why, but I do know I have to be obedient to God, so here, take this." If your praise was silent yesterday, how can you keep quiet now? There is a current of praise that has just swelled up inside of you and it's got to come out. Sometimes you just need to be reminded of the many things that God has done for you. It will bring you back in alignment with your praise and back on the road of grace and thanksgiving.

Praise keeps you glad. It changes your way of thinking. An old saying states, "No gratitude is a bad attitude," but I would like to add: "Gratitude brings forth praise which results in a good attitude!"

I believe some days God gets out His "Book of Remembrance." What's in His "Book of Remembrance?" Since He is attracted to praise, I believe He begins to recall your praises one by one. Perhaps God's eyes become a little moist as He reads His chronicle of your praises. You've just touched His soft spot. God says, "I need to send favor to her today. Her

A Book of Remembrance

285

praises logged in the heavenly 'Book of Remembrance' have brought honor to Me. I'm going to send her a blessing!" He gives the assignment to Jesus who then goes to the Holy Spirit and says, "Orders from the King—carry out this assignment. God's favor is ready to be delivered to planet earth." The Holy Spirit arrives at your front door and says, "Special delivery from the King, one box full of heaven's blessings!"

Suddenly, unexpectedly, your joy increases, you feel physically stronger, your child's fever breaks, your mate tells you he is sorry, the phone rings offering you a new job, your backslidden daughter gets saved. Little did you know your praise had been recorded in heaven and God had to send *you* a "thank you!"

This reminds me again of the story of Esther. Unable to sleep, King Xerxes was flipping through some records in the royal archives. In the Royal Books of Remembrance, King Xerxes read of the assassination plot that Mordecai thwarted. Surprised to learn that Mordecai had never been rewarded for this deed, the king asked Haman what should be done to properly thank a hero. Haman thought the king must be talking about himself, and so he described a lavish reward. The king agreed, but to Haman's shock and utter humiliation, he learned that Mordecai—his enemy—was the person to be so honored! The words scripted in the royal journal when reread brought to remembrance something that had been overlooked. The words penned to the pages leaped off and Mordecai found favor with the king.

Your praises written on a piece of paper may sound simple and elementary to you, but when you reflect back upon them, or perhaps when they are read by the next generation, they could be as powerful as the words read by King Xerxes the night he could not sleep.

Lord, help me to get past my past, but don't let me forget all that You have brought me through either! Bring to remembrance those things that bring You glory and for which I should continually praise You! Don't let me forget all the amazing things You have revealed to me, and especially all the fiery trials through which You have proven Yourself faithful.

One Minute of Praise:

Begin your "Book or Remembrance" by taking the next minute to write down something God has shown you today.

_____

_____

_____

_____

_____

_____

A Book of Remembrance

You can always praise God one minute for:

- Drawing you to prayer and power
- The salvation of your soul
- Sending the Holy Spirit
- Producing spiritual gifts in your life
- The fruit of the Spirit working in you
- The wonderful gift of praise
- All the ways He has intervened in your affairs
- His divine plan for your life
- How He will never leave you nor forsake you
- Bringing you to a place of maturity and fuller life
- Lifting you up when you fall
- Keeping you in perfect peace
- Making all things work together for your good
- Protecting you from the snares of your enemy
- The wonder-working power in His Word and in the blood of the Lamb
- Giving His angels charge over you
- Fighting for you against your adversaries
- Making you more than a conqueror

- Supplying all your needs according to His riches in glory

- His healing power upon your body, soul, and spirit

- Flooding your heart with the light of heaven

- Always causing you to triumph in Christ Jesus

- Turning your curses into blessings

- Enabling you to dwell in safety

- All the blessings of life

- His greatness, power, glory, majesty, splendor, and righteousness

- Silencing your enemies

- Because He is at your right hand and you shall not be moved

- He is trustworthy

- Not allowing your enemies to rejoice over you

- His wonderful love

- He is great and greatly to be praised

- Delivering your soul from death and your feet from stumbling

- He is your fortress and refuge in times of trouble

- His faithfulness and marvelous deeds

You can always praise God one minute for:

- His acts of power and surpassing greatness

- Dispersing spiritual blindness from your spirit

- Lifting you out of the depths

- Preserving you and keeping your feet from slipping

- The name of the Lord being a strong tower so the righteous can run into it and be safe

But most of all . . .

- Just thank Him for Who He is!

About the Author

*D*arlene McCarty, known as **"The Bee Lady"**, was born March 4, 1950, in Littlefield, Texas, to Rev. Loyd and Mary Walker, ordained ministers with the Foursquare Church. At the age of six, Darlene was diagnosed with rheumatic fever, which left her with a seriously damaged heart. The doctors said she would never live to see her 21st birthday. She could not play like normal children and even had to be carried up steps. At the age of 10, God miraculously healed her heart, which today is still in perfect condition. From the day that she was born as a five-pound premature baby and not expected to live, God has had His almighty and protective hand on her life.

At the age of 14, Darlene attended her first church camp in Roaring Springs, Texas. This was her first and only camp to be privileged to attend, but God had a purpose for that time. At the altar of this Assembly of God camp, God placed a calling upon her life that still burns deep in her soul. She stayed in the altar with a counselor until 4:00 a.m. having a conversation with the Lord. God was preparing her for what she was about to face in three months; an event that would affect the rest of her life. That devastating event took place on October 23, 1964, when her dad suffered a fatal heart attack at home, leaving her and her mom all alone. The local Baptist Church in this small community opened a trust fund for Darlene's college education.

After graduating from high school, she was able to attend Southwestern Assemblies of God University in Waxahachie, Texas, because of the kindness of her small community. She met her husband, Randel, while attending college and they were married June 6, 1970. While attending college, they took their first youth pastor's position in Athens, Texas. Since that time, they have pastored in Alabama and Tennessee.

In 1979, Randel and Darlene were asked to accept the position of President of College and Career Ministries for the Tennessee District of the Assemblies of God. For 13 years they lived in Nashville ministering to over 40,000 teenagers. Wherever they travel, they always met someone that was associated with their ministry during those years.

For the past 20 years they have ministered in churches and crusades in Chili, Ecuador, Columbia, Honduras, Costa

Rica, Bahamas, Jamaica, Mexico, Thailand, Hong Kong, Korea, Philippines, Russia and the United States. She and her husband continue to travel across the United States and other countries reaching out to the hurting with much compassion.

In 1990 they accepted the senior pastor position at Cathedral of Praise in Memphis, Tennessee. In 2005 they celebrated their 15th Anniversary at Cathedral of Praise and 35 years of ministry. Under their leadership, the congregation grew from 100 to over 700. In June of 1996, they visited Brownsville Assembly of God Church in Pensacola, Florida, and had a life-changing experience. On Father's Day of 1996, revival came to Cathedral of Praise like a mighty flood. The flow of the "River" has brought renewing, repenting, healing, and lives being restored. God's glory has engulfed their church.

Darlene has received a mighty anointed touch from God that has changed her from a quiet, subdued woman that loved God to a radical fanatic for the Lord. A new boldness took her out of her comfort zone and forced her into a spiritual war zone doing battle with Satan. The mantle that God has placed upon her is evident to anyone sitting under her ministry. *The **Spirit of the Lord** has called her to bring forth the Word to bind up the brokenhearted, proclaim liberty to the captives, release darkness for the prisoners, proclaim the year of the Lord's favor, and comfort those who mourn.*

About the Author 293

Her book, *"Glory from the Honeycomb"*, has been read by thousands. Reading this book will birth a new desire in your spirit to see God's glorious presence. She is presently writing two books, one called "Erasing Scars" that will contain her life-changing testimony and a number of dreams and visions that God has given her since 1996 pertaining to healing past hurts and wounds and the other a "One Minute of Praise" Devotional Journal.

God birthed a unique ministry in her in 1997 about **"Bee All God Created You To Bee"**. *Eat Thou Honey Ministries* was formed with a line of jewelry called *"The Honeycomb Collection"*. Women and men all over the world wear her pins using them as a witnessing tool, sharing Jesus to a lost generation. These pins open conversations that open doors to share with others their faith in God. Timid people become bold, shy people become a conversationalist. All this by wearing a beautiful pin with a few rhinestones that receives a compliment such as: "That is a beautiful pin you are wearing". And you say, "Thank you, I wear this as a reminder to *Bee All God Created Me To Bee!*" Each pin has a name, scripture and application. Something so small, but so powerful!

In November of 1997, she hosted her first *"Eat Thou Honey"* **Ladies' Conference** at Cathedral of Praise where she and her husband are senior pastors. It began with a few hundred and now has over 1,300 in attendance. Five Spirit-filled speakers, filled with power and anointing, minister to hungry women each year. Speakers such as Brenda Kilpatrick, Judy Jacobs, Lila Terhune, Ruth Heflin, Peggy Richards, Dr. Juanita Bynum, Dianne Sloan, Suzanne Hinn, Varle Rollins, Beverly Bilbo, Karen Wheaton, Pastor Darlene Bishop, Tommy Tenney, Martha Munizzi, Valerie Boyd, and Pastor Paula White have been a part of this conference.

On January 14, 1999, Grace Christian Fellowship of Memphis, Tennessee, honored women in leadership such as: Doctors, Lawyers, Judges, Free Lance Writer, Authors, Ministers, etc. These women of Memphis were nominated for their strength and ability to build future success, mentoring people who need it most, and helping others overcome defeat. Darlene was a recipient of this **"Life Changing '99 Award"**.

For the past 12 months Darlene has been ministering on the ***"Power of Praise"***. If the enemy can get your praise, he has your mind, which opens doors to taking over the soul man and the spirit man. She engraves in women's hearts the words found in Ps 8:2, Ps 3:7, and Is 41:15 & 16. Start your day out with ***"One Minute of Praise!"*** No asking for anything, just praising Him. Your praise will silence your enemy, break his jaw bone, and shatter his teeth. God will take your praise, tear all your enemies apart, making chaff of your mountain, then toss it in the air! Lives are being changed; women are set free by the powerful message.

Pastor Darlene has ministered with Bishop T.D. Jakes, Serita Jakes, Pilar Sanders, Dr. Wanda Turner, Elder Debra

Morton, Darlene Bishop, Paula White, Charlyn Singleton, Judy Jacobs, Reba McQuire, Shirley Arnold, and Heidi Baker to name a few. This year she has also had the privilege to minister at **The RAMP** for Karen Wheaton, appeared on TBN in May as a guest of Prophetess Juanita Bynum and in June as a guest of Pastor Paula White, ministered at a Pastor's Conference in the Philippines, and preached at a Women's Conference in Russia with over 5,000 in attendance, was a guest speaker at Juanita Bynum's "*Women on the Frontline*" ladies conference in Tampa, Florida, plus many other ladies conferences across the nation.

Darlene and Randel have pastored Cathedral of Praise in Memphis, Tennessee for 16 years. They have two children, Tyra 32 and Tiffany 25 and they are the proud grandparents of Mackenzie Ashlyn Whitehurst, 7 years old, and Chase Walker Whitehurst, born December 22, 2002 and passed away April 24, 2006. Tyra and her husband Jason, serve as senior pastors at Music City Assembly of God in Nashville, Tennessee. Tiffany and her husband Paul are children's pastors at Cathedral of Praise. Tiffany also serves as the multi-media director. They have one son Cole Anthony Strong who was born on October 10, 2005.

Darlene McCarty

"The Bee Lady"

Cathedral of Praise Assemblies of God Church

P.O. Box 2108, Cordova, TN 38088 (Ch)

P. O. Box 700, Cordova, TN 38088 (Off)

CH: (901)755-1540 / HM OFF: (901)757-1994

FAX: (901)737-7953

E-mail: darlene@darlenemccarty.com

Web Site: www.darlenemccarty.com

About the Author

Endnotes

1. Jamieson, Fausset, and Brown Commentary, Electronic Database. Copyright © 1997, 2003 by Biblesoft, Inc. All rights reserved.

2. Tenney, Tommy, *Finding Favor with the King*, Bethany House, Bloomington, Minnesota, 2003.

3. Picket, Fuchsia, *Worship Him*, pg. 119-120.

4. Heinrichs, Marcyne, pg. 121.

5. Zschech, Darlene, *Extravagant Worship*, Check Music Ministries, Castle Hill, Australia, 2001.

6. Brock, Bobby C., *A Passion for His Presence*, iUniverse, Inc., Lincoln, NE, 2004.

7. Ibid, 47.